Surprised by God

Lives turned upside down

Faith Cook

EP BOOKS

Faverdale North

Darlington

DL3 oPH, England

web: http://www.epbooks.org

e-mail: sales@epbooks.org

EP Books are distributed in the USA by:

JPL Distribution

3741 Linden Avenue Southeast

Grand Rapids, MI 49548

E-mail: orders@jpldistribution.com

Tel: 877.683.6935

First published 2002 as *Lives Turned Upside Down* (*Champions of the faith*), ISBN 978–0–85234–521–4

This revised edition published 2014

ISBN: 978–1–78397–008–7

British Library Cataloguing in Publication Data available

All Scripture quotes are from the New King James Version, unless otherwise noted.

'These who have turned the world upside down have come here too'   (Acts 17:6, NKJV).

Christ's gospel does turn the world upside down.
It was the wrong way upwards before,
but when the gospel shall prevail
It will set the world right by turning it upside down.

C. H. Spurgeon

To my grandchildren:
Liz, Emily, Susanna, Sam,
Charlotte, Ben, Daniel, Hannah, Trinity and Scarlett.

Contents

William Mackay

The doctor's Bible

Although trained as a doctor, William P. Mackay, born in Montrose, Scotland in 1839, became a highly-acknowledged preacher and writer. His sixteen years' ministry in Hull, East Yorkshire, was cut short by his death in an accident in 1885.

William Mackay

The doctor's Bible

It was 1856 and seventeen-year-old William Mackay was about to leave his home in Montrose, Scotland to start his medical studies in Edinburgh. An ambitious and intelligent young man, he was eagerly anticipating his future career, but as his mother helped William pack his belongings, she felt a dart of anxiety. Would her son remember the faith that his parents had taught him over the years or would he quickly adopt the ways and attitudes of his fellow students? Carefully she slipped a parting gift into William's trunk—a Bible, inscribing it with her son's name and with her own. Underneath Mrs Mackay added a verse of scripture as a beacon to guide the young man through the maze of temptations and snares which might so easily entangle him.

Despising the Scriptures

Quickly absorbed into his new surroundings and studies, William paid little attention to his mother's gift. Day after day the Bible lay in his room neglected, its pages unopened, its warnings unheeded. The friends he made were very different from the company he remembered from his childhood. These men had little time for those truths and principles that William had been taught to respect. Unbelieving and cynical, they looked with contempt on anyone who held what they considered to be long outmoded ideas. Soon William, too, started to throw off any lingering pangs of conscience and to spurn the faith he had learnt at home. Like his peers he began to drink indulgently and would frequently be seen with a tot of whisky in his hand whether he was studying or socializing. Gradually drink became his master, until his slim student finances could scarcely indulge his habit.

Then came a day when William had no money left to finance his craving. His mind turned to the three golden balls that hung temptingly outside the nearest pawnshop. What could he pawn to buy himself a little more whisky? He glanced round his room. His eyes fell on the Bible his mother had given him. He blew off the dust and turned it over carefully in his hand. Little used, it should fetch a good price, and of course he would redeem it one day, he told himself. At least it would meet his present needs. Hardening his conscience against any remembrance of the one who had lovingly inscribed both his name and hers on its flyleaf, the medical student took the Bible to the local pawnshop.

All thoughts of the Bible soon faded from his mind, however, as William became engrossed in his work, his friends and his prospects. The years passed and eventually, despite his whisky drinking habits, the young man graduated with high honours in his medical studies, and before long gained a prominent position in an Edinburgh hospital. Now he freely and publicly disparaged the faith he had been taught in his youth. The God in whom his mother trusted was held up as a subject for ridicule and unbelieving jokes. More than this Mackay became a leading member of a society known as the Infidel Club. His rejection of God quickly led to a rejection of the moral standards that God's Word demanded, as William Mackay yielded to all the pressures around him, becoming dissolute and profligate in his lifestyle.

Fighting death

One aspect of his work, however, gave the young doctor unusual satisfaction, but not for the right reasons. With no belief in God, he delighted to pit his medical skill against humanity's final and last enemy: death itself. When he could drag a patient back from the very gates of death, he would revel in his conquest, for it proved, or so he thought, that by his own innate ability, he could be master of his own destiny. Whenever he heard the rattle of a cart turning into the hospital gates, bringing in another victim of some tragic accident, the adrenalin began to flow. Dr Mackay gloried in a further opportunity to demonstrate his superior powers over the course of nature. Once more he would be the centre of an admiring circle of colleagues, all congratulating him on his incredible achievement.

Then came a day when, with a flurry of activity in the hospital, yet another man, critically injured probably in some industrial accident, was admitted to the ward. The lower half of his body was horribly crushed—he could not have many hours to live. Again William Mackay hastened to the scene—surely the right man to deal with such a situation. The victim was in desperate pain, but one thing startled the doctor. He had observed the faces of many as they lay wracked with agony from multiple injuries, but there was a strange look on this man's face—a serenity that defied explanation.

'What's the diagnosis, doctor?' asked the injured man.

'Oh, I guess we will pull you through,' replied Mackay cheerily.

'No, doctor, I don't want any guess. I want to know if it is life or death.' Mackay looked at his patient with astonishment. 'Just lay me down easy. Anywhere, doctor,' the patient continued. His voice was growing weaker. 'I am ready. I am not afraid to die. I trust in the precious shed blood of the Lord Jesus Christ. If I have to die, I know I am going to be with him. But I would like to know the truth; just what is my condition?'

Able to cope with most contingencies, William Mackay scarcely knew how to answer this calm-faced man. Then he blurted out the truth, 'You have at the most three hours to live.'

'Thank you, doctor,' replied the dying man quietly. Even the hardened and cynical medic was suddenly touched.

'Is there anything special you would like us to do for you?' he asked kindly.

'In one of my pockets is a two-week's pay packet,' replied his patient. 'Please could someone take it at once to my landlady to pay for my lodgings. And, yes, there is one more thing. Could you ask her to send me the book?'

'What book is that?' asked the surprised doctor.

'Oh, just the book,' the man replied faintly. 'She'll know.'

As he carried on his duties around the hospital, William Mackay could not erase the sight of that calm face. Nor could he shut out the sound of those words, 'I am ready, doctor. Just lay me down easy. Anywhere. I am ready.' Ready for death? This was a concept that Mackay had long since rejected from his code of life. Normally able to shrug off even the most appalling scenes of human suffering, the doctor felt he must know what had happened to his patient. Did he get his book before he died? Rarely would Mackay return to a ward once he had accepted that his patient was dying. But now he broke his usual rule and surprised the nurse in charge by arriving back at the ward and asking after the casualty he had placed under her care. 'He died a few minutes ago,' was her simple reply.

'And did he get his book?' enquired the doctor. 'What was it? A bank book?'

'Yes, he got his book,' answered the nurse. 'It arrived shortly before he died. But no, it wasn't his bank book. It is still there, under his pillow, if you want to look at it.'

Confronted

Reaching the dead man's bedside, the doctor felt under the pillow and pulled out the book. It was a Bible. It looked strangely familiar. He opened it. And there on the flyleaf he was startled to read his own name, and the name of his mother, together with the scripture text she had given him so long ago. This was the very Bible he had pawned for whisky as a student. With shocked shame, Mackay thrust the Bible under his coat and hurried to his private office. Choking with emotion he fell on his knees and begged God to forgive his sins and have mercy upon him.

Dr William Mackay was a man in debt—a debt to the unexpected mercy of God and a debt to the men and women of his generation whose faith he had deluded and mocked. How could he repay such a debt? To his God he could repay nothing, but with a zeal born of gratitude he could give his life in the service of others, seeking to make good the damage he had done and the wasted years. Whenever he had opportunity, he spoke to his friends, his associates, to anyone who would listen, telling them of God's mercy to a sinner.

William Mackay's Bible was no longer neglected as he became an earnest student of its pages. When its limp covers wore out, he had the book carefully rebound in hardback covers, doubly precious now because of its associations.

A gift for preaching

Soon it became apparent that the young doctor had a remarkable gift for preaching the profound truths of the gospel with a simplicity that even the most untaught could understand. Requests began to pour in from all over the area for his services at preaching meetings. He found himself unable to combine such commitments with his medical work and in 1869 William Mackay, now twenty-nine years of age, decided to turn his back on all the accolades of a successful medical career and enter the Christian ministry. As he responded to invitations from various churches to preach for them, one in particular attracted his attention. In Hull a newly-formed and struggling Presbyterian cause with only twenty-four members asked him if he would become their pastor. Other churches were also offering him their pulpits, some far more influential. But to Hull he went. The members were not able to support him adequately and so he decided to take no fixed income. A box was placed at the back of the church for members to donate as much as they felt able to give. The work grew steadily and, for the next sixteen years, William Mackay served the people of Hull, preaching the gospel with an ardour that more than compensated for the wasted years.

As the congregations increased, the need for better premises became apparent. Soon the church moved from a side road to a prominent building in Prospect Street, one of Hull's main thoroughfares at the time. Still Mackay refused to take any settled income, wishing the members to give as much aid as possible to missionary endeavour. Other churches in Hull were also encouraged by his ministry—for this was a city full of churches, a city that had known remarkable blessings from God in the past. Hull was not the only place to benefit from the preaching of William Mackay.

Tirelessly he responded to calls from north and south alike. Travelling in days when trains were still slow and far from comfortable, the earnest preacher could be found in London, Dublin and Perth, and even in America, preaching the gospel he had once despised. In the first six months of 1875 alone Mackay had covered more than 6,000 miles by train, reaching the farthest corners of the British Isles. But whenever possible he would be back in Hull for the Sunday services even if it meant arriving home in the early hours of the morning.

'En Hakkore'

And always William Mackay's old Bible was an invariable companion on all his long journeys. Its pages, now blackened with constant thumbing as he read and reread them, were heavily underlined, the ink lines criss-crossing each other as he linked together passages of particular significance to him. And to his Bible, with all its unforgettable memories, he gave a special and unexpected name. He called it 'En Hakkore'. This strange name comes from the book of Judges and was chosen by Samson to commemorate God's intervention on his behalf in the aftermath of his extraordinary victory over the Philistines. Battle-weary, Samson had thought he would die of thirst unless God should miraculously supply his need. When God opened up a bubbling spring of water for the thirsty warrior, Samson called the place En Hakkore (Judges 15:18). So too when William Mackay, weary and thirsty in the battle of life, called on God to refresh his soul, he discovered a spring of living water close at hand. And that fountain where he could drink in abundance had its source within the pages of his Bible. What better name could he give it than En Hakkore?

Marriage and the birth of his sons enriched Mackay's home but did not deflect him from the sole purpose for which he now lived. With a naturally buoyant and hopeful spirit, his presence always cheered and encouraged those with whom he mingled. That intellect that had formerly been employed to bring honour to his own name was now devoted to making the truths of the gospel transparently clear to everyone who heard him preach. With a masterly gift for homely illustration, he clarified even the most obscure subjects, yet without robbing the truths of God's Word of their profundity.

Whenever it became known that William Mackay was due to preach in a locality, the crowds would gather. One who heard him spoke of the preacher's 'intense zeal for the honour of Christ and his tender yearning for the souls of the people'. Concerned for all his hearers, both for unbelievers and those who professed to be Christians, his message was always succinct and startling: 'If ever I utter the words *I think*,' he declared on one occasion, 'I hope the people will go to sleep and remain asleep until I have done with *thinking*. We are not here to give our *thoughts*, but God's words.' Manly and forceful in his style, Mackay always evoked a response from his congregation. Preaching on one occasion on 'The claims of the Man, Jesus', he cried out rhetorically to his crowded congregation, 'Who here believes in this rejected Man?' In almost involuntary response, hundreds rose to their feet from all parts of the building to declare their allegiance to the Man of Sorrows.

Grace and truth

Although he recognized the supreme value of preaching as God's chosen way to reach out to the unbeliever, Mackay also realized the part to be played by the printed page. Between his journeys and his preaching engagements he began to write up the sermons which he felt would best influence those who might never attend a regular church service. For ten years he worked at his small volume, always trying to improve it, until at last he ventured to send his first book, *Grace and Truth*, to the publishers. Marked by the simplicity as well as the depth and insight of his preaching style, this unassuming book of twelve sermons became widely sought after. Within five years it had been translated into many languages and had sold nearly a quarter of a million copies. After ten years it had run into fifty-eight editions. 'I do not hesitate to say that I have seen no book so likely to do good for many a long day,' wrote J. C. Ryle, then Bishop of Liverpool, while C. H. Spurgeon could echo, 'It is full of gospel truth—dropping with it, like the honeycomb and honey.' Even today *Grace and Truth* may be found on many bookseller's list of secondhand books, carefully inscribed with its first owner's name. Two more books of sermons would follow, *Abundant Grace* and *The Seeking Saviour*, both published after Mackay's death.

Although robust and energetic, William Mackay perhaps sensed the limitations of his strength, fearing that his own days might be cut short and his opportunities for preaching that gospel of grace and truth curtailed by illness. Certainly he felt the need of some place of retreat from the ceaseless demands on his time and strength even though he was only in his mid-forties. Early in the 1880s Mackay and his wife had a small villa built for themselves in Oban, north-west Scotland, where they could go for short holidays—although 'a holiday' would be a misnomer. As soon as it became known that Mackay had arrived, requests for him to preach poured in from all sides—requests that he found impossible to refuse. Preaching in Oban one Sunday evening in the late summer of 1885, Mackay took as his subject 'The glory of God'. He scarcely knew how to stop as he described the surpassing glory of God revealed above all in his Son, Jesus Christ, but also glimpsed by privileged men and women in the pages of Scripture. Who could stand in the light of that glory? he asked. Could Moses, Job, Isaiah, Ezekiel or the apostle John? No, they all fell down before such transcendent majesty. How then can we poor sinners hope to stand …? Time was ticking away and Mackay seemed almost in the glory himself. He had more to say, but would have to draw to a close. Before he did so, however, he invited his congregation to return the following Sunday to hear the rest of his sermon.

Beholding his glory

But they never heard it. Before that day arrived William Mackay himself was standing in the presence of the God of glory. On the Monday of that week he had decided on a trip by steamer from Oban to Thurso, sailing to the far north of Scotland between desolate and beautiful islands. Calling at Portree on the way, Mackay, together with other passengers, alighted for a short walk along the pier. The light was failing and the pier was treacherous. He missed his footing, slipped and fell into the sea below, striking his head on the bow of the steamer as he fell. Rescued from the water, William Mackay was unconscious as he was carried to a nearby hotel. There he rallied, and had one request to make. Expecting to make a full recovery, he asked that his wife and children, who had not accompanied him, should not be told about his accident. The recovery was only transient, however, and the next night a congestion of the lungs brought his short ministry of only sixteen years to a premature close. When his wife arrived the next day she could only say, 'He has entered the pearly gates and is beholding his glory.'

Continued blessing

But the story of William Mackay is not quite done. Even though the voice of the preacher might be silenced in death, the written word continued to point countless numbers of men and women to the one who had indeed conquered the power of death—as Mackay himself had tried to do before his own conversion. Two instances must suffice. The first is of James Hannington, a missionary martyred in Uganda only weeks after Mackay himself died. Some years previously as a young candidate for ordination, Hannington was fearful in case he himself might be a stranger to the very truths he was supposed to be preaching. A recently converted friend was also concerned for him and sent him a copy of Mackay's book, *Grace and Truth*, together with an account of his own spiritual experience. Hannington tried to read the book, but threw it down in disgust. Then he realized he must answer his friend's letter, so tried to read it once more. This time it annoyed him so much that he flung the offending book across the room. Yet how could he write to his friend unless he tried once more? Picking 'the old thing' up some weeks later, he read on until he reached the fourth chapter which was headed, 'Do you feel your sins forgiven?' As he read Hannington began to understand what he was reading. He leapt up, rejoicing that at last he had found the answer to his long quest. Now he knew his sins were forgiven: Jesus had died for him.

The second instance, seventy-five years later, is of a young Inverness dentist who was deeply unhappy. Like William Mackay himself, Donald had been privileged to have a Christian home and parents who had taught him to value Christian truth from earliest days. Although he had not rejected the faith, he had not responded to it either. Orderly and dutiful in his conduct, he would scarcely have considered himself a sinner like the common and unprincipled types among whom he mingled daily.

Such thinking came to an abrupt end on 11 January 1959. A sermon preached by a Donald MacDonald, minister of Greyfriars Free Church in Inverness, profoundly disturbed the young dentist. The preacher informed him that he too, upright and honourable though he considered himself to be, was heading for judgement. Dismayed, the trainee dentist returned to his lodgings. Where could he find an answer to the new fears that were now haunting him? Then he remembered that his landlady owned some religious books. Rooting round in the cupboard, Donald discovered a slim red volume written in the previous century called *Grace and Truth*. Pulling it out, he opened its pages and the very first chapter gripped his attention. It bore the title 'There is no difference', and the writer, a certain W. P. Mackay, a name quite unknown to Donald, showed with pithy and unerring clarity that no one is good enough in the sight of God to obtain salvation by his own merits. Here was further testimony to the young dentist telling him of his lost condition. Donald read and reread the book until it became the means of bringing yet another to seek salvation through the merits of Jesus Christ. Relating his story many years later after a lifetime in the Christian ministry, Donald still gladly owns his debt to William Mackay, the Scottish preacher from Hull.

Words of a hymn written by William Mackay express his own sense of the saving mercy of God and the gratitude that motivated him in all his endeavour:

All glory and praise
To the Lamb that was slain,
Who has borne all our sins
And has cleansed every stain.

All glory and praise
To the God of all grace
Who has bought us and taught us
And shown us his grace.

Hallelujah! thine the glory,
Hallelujah! we sing;
Hallelujah! thine the glory,
Our praise now we bring.

New Christian Hymns No. 56

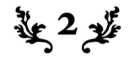

William Clowes

'A burning and a shining light'

The Primitive Methodist Connexion sprang from the vision and zeal of a group of young men in the English Potteries. It separated from the main Wesleyan Methodist Church in 1812. William Clowes, together with Hugh Bourne, was the acknowledged leader in this new work of the Spirit of God.

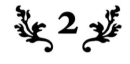

William Clowes

'A burning and a shining light'

It was only six o'clock in the morning, but ten-year-old William Clowes was already hard at work. Standing in his uncle's pottery shed, he had a twelve-hour day ahead of him, learning the trade of a master potter. William was directly descended from Josiah Wedgwood, of pottery fame, and had already shown an early aptitude for the family business. He had mastered the art of dividing and tossing the clay to achieve the correct blend and had learnt the intricacies of moulding the delicate figurines for which Wedgwood pottery had become renowned. As he turned the shapely jars and plates on the wheel, the boy's accurate work showed that he had inherited the family skills to a marked degree.

Early training

Born in Burslem in Staffordshire in March 1780, William could boast that his great grandfather, Josiah, had built the largest house in Burslem half a century earlier. But Samuel Clowes, William's own father, who had married Ann Wedgwood, was a waster. So for William himself there was only a poverty-stricken hovel where his hard-working mother struggled to keep the family out of debt. Any money his father earned was quickly dissipated on drink and gambling. The few pence that William could add to the family budget each week were urgently needed to boost the finances. In time, however, the boy's ability earned him some extra pay which he used to augment his previously inadequate education by attending night school.

As William Clowes matured it became evident that he was a natural leader. Medium in build, well-proportioned and athletic, he combined unusual physical strength with a magnetic personality, and quickly gained status as a role-model for the village boys of Burslem. With his apprenticeship completed, William soon attained to the status of master craftsman—a position which commanded a high-earning potential. It would seem that the youth was set for a successful career. Dominant and cheerful as he was, there was also a reflective side to his nature. He could later recall weeping inconsolably over his sins at some religious meeting, even as a ten-year-old.

Dancing, running, long jump, boxing: William Clowes excelled at them all. But he lacked one thing: strong parental guidance and discipline. The example set by his indolent and self-indulgent father did nothing to encourage William to channel his gifts and abilities towards any constructive end. Dancing became his favourite pastime, and before long he could add to his list of achievements many accolades as a prize dancer. He won national awards for the competitions he entered and soon there were few in the entire country who could compete with the boy from Burslem for poise and proficiency on the dance floor. But with the dancing came the inevitable accompaniments of alcohol and gambling. These, coupled with an easy vulgarity and profanity, marred his life.

Deep conviction

Yet always, despite a hardened exterior, the quiet voice of conscience protested constantly against his way of life. Even the noise of the musical instruments in the dance hall could not drown its incessant whisper at times: 'For all these things you will surely be brought to judgement,' it seemed to be warning. Then terror would seize hold of William until he managed to silence the accusing voice with yet more alcohol. One night as he danced the small hours away in Burslem Town Hall, the sense of impending condemnation gained the mastery to such an extent that he suddenly turned and fled from the hall. Thinking that their son had been suddenly taken ill, his parents dosed him with gin and tobacco until he was physically sick as well. In an agony of fear he begged his mother to pray for him. Dutiful though she was, Ann Clowes could not help. At last, vowing urgently to serve God for the rest of his life, the young man found rest in sleep.

This experience was not quickly forgotten. From this time on William's life was built around efforts to reform his ways, punctuated by interludes of wild, boisterous behaviour. Would marriage help him to become steadier, he wondered? So, at twenty years of age, he courted and married Hannah Rogers. Hannah's friends warned her against the consequences of marrying such a tempestuous firebrand as Clowes, but she was deaf to their entreaties. Even William himself was uncertain about the step he was taking and later confessed that on the day of his wedding he nearly decided to leave Hannah alone in the aisle and make a quick escape. Predictably his marriage brought no lasting reformation leaving him yet more acutely aware of his sins. At last his mental distress became unbearable as his behaviour grew increasingly erratic. Once he broke down and wept uncontrollably in front of Hannah making her fear for his sanity. Dismayed, she suggested that the answer to his problems was not weeping or praying but a life of industry and self-control—the very thing Clowes could not achieve. Yet despite all this, he continued to make progress in the pottery industry. Now he could even earn a whole pound in a single day—at a time when most could scarcely earn that much in a week.

Desertion

After several years of stormy married life, Clowes suddenly took offence at something Hannah had done. Losing his temper, he struck the wall violently and marched out of the house taking with him nothing but his mother's Prayer Book. Penniless, he wandered some forty miles reading his Prayer Book, weeping and wondering at the strange course his life had taken. At last he reached Warrington and decided to settle there and seek employment. Still the inner conflict went on. Again and again he would vow to God that he would reform his life. 'Sometimes,' as he later wrote in his journal, 'I used to walk in solitary and unfrequented places, wishing that I was a bird or a beast, or anything that was not accountable to the tribunal of heaven.'

Leaving Warrington, the restless man soon set off on his travels again. This time he decided to make his home in Hull. Once more he obtained an excellent job, yet still his former habits gained the mastery over him. Drink and bad company inflamed all the old passions. Even though Hull would become the scene of some of his most disgraceful behaviour, God, who sees the heart had not forsaken the dissolute young man. These were the days when press gangs roamed the streets on the look-out for lazy idlers. Grabbing them suddenly from behind they forced their captives into military service. What better escapade, thought Clowes, than to impersonate a press-gang officer and frighten some of the customers at the local taverns? Dressed in the typical gear of such an official, complete with its gaudy yellow buttons, Clowes and his friends raided their old haunts, and only released the victims when they had had the satisfaction of seeing their terror-struck faces. But it was a double-edged joke. One day as Clowes was wasting his time in a tavern in the quiet village of Barton-on-Humber, a ferry trip across the Humber estuary, some genuine press-gang men seized him as he was involved in a drunken brawl.

Only when his master pleaded for him was Clowes set free. The scare made him resolve to seek the refuge of his home once more, and soon he began the long trudge of over a hundred and thirty miles back to Burslem. Again he read his Prayer Book as he travelled. Turning to prayers to be used at the Communion service, his eyes suddenly fell on words he had never noticed before: 'They that eat and drink [of the Lord's Supper] unworthily, eat and drink damnation to themselves.'

The Love-Feast

'What a shocking sin!' thought Clowes. Hardly had he reached home before he was invited to attend a service at the Methodist church. Yes, he would go, he thought, even though something known as a 'lovefeast' was to follow. Clowes accepted a ticket for the celebration from a friend, scarcely knowing what happened at such occasions. Each ticket bore a name, for only members of that particular Methodist Society were allowed to attend the lovefeast. Someone stood at the door inspecting tickets so that no non-member could enter. Holding his thumb over all but the first letter of his friend's name—a name that also began with 'C'—Clowes hoped to steal in.

As the official took the ticket from Clowes' hand to examine it a sudden gust of wind blew out the candle. Another candle was called for. But as the ticket inspector took the ticket once more a further puff of wind blew the second candle out. 'Move on,' said he impatiently, waving Clowes forward, for others were waiting. When members of the society began to share a simple meal, consisting of plain cake and water, Clowes assumed, wrongly in fact, that this must be a Communion service. He began to tremble involuntarily, recollecting the judgement of God on those who eat or drink unworthily. 'If I sin once more,' thought William, 'my damnation is forever sealed.' Returning home he told Hannah of his new resolve to act the part of a Christian.

A changed life

As good as his word, twenty-five-year-old Clowes turned up for the seven o'clock prayer meeting on the following day. As he knelt he secretly pleaded with God to help him in his new determination to lead a perfect life. Then he became conscious of a strange and inexplicable influence stealing over him. 'What is this,' he wondered? And then he answered his own question: 'This is what the Methodists mean by being converted. Yes, this is it! God is converting my soul.' Later he recorded: 'I felt my bands breaking. In an agony of soul I believed God *would* save me—then I believed he *was* saving me—then I believed he *had* saved me; and it was so.' 'God has pardoned all my sins,' he confided to someone afterwards. The news spread round the building like a flame. All present fell to their knees and thanked God for the wonder of his saving mercy.

Clowes now found he had an inner strength to change his ways. He paid his debts, turned his back on the dance hall and re-ordered his home life to give priority to spiritual concerns. He began to pray urgently for Hannah. Great was his joy when she too was converted not many weeks later; both became members of the Burslem Methodist Society. His former friends and workmates thought him mad, but regardless of their sneers, he testified of God's mercy wherever he went. In fact Clowes was at last truly sane. With a 'burning sympathy' for the souls of others, he and Hannah opened their home for times of prayer and testimony. Soon the Burslem house became too small for all who wished to crowd in, so they moved to roomier accommodation in nearby Tunstall.

Among the many who visited the Clowes home one day was a shy, intense man named Hugh Bourne. Brought up on a moorland farm several miles north of Tunstall, Bourne had known years of inner anguish because of his sense of sin. With no one to guide him to the Saviour who alone could atone for his sin, Bourne had at last found relief as he read a moving work by the old Methodist preacher, John Fletcher, from nearby Madeley. 'I never knew or thought that anyone could in this world have such a foretaste of heaven,' exclaimed Hugh Bourne as he tried to describe the joys he now felt. This had taken place in 1799, six years before Clowes himself had been converted.

Painfully shy though he was, Bourne could not stop himself from seeking to influence his friends and had gathered around him a small group of men each with a heart aflame for the salvation of others. News of the change in Clowes drew Bourne to seek out his company. Long into the night they spoke together with fervent eagerness of all God's dealings with them.

All unknown to either of them, right there, in the heart of the English Potteries, a nucleus of men whom God was going to use in an unusual way was being formed. Bourne introduced Clowes to his other friends: miners, potters, farmers—none well-educated or extraordinarily gifted, but each anxious to touch their generation with the message of the transforming grace of God. Now they were longing to reach the people, but what else could they do?

Camp meetings

Just as they were wondering about this, they discovered that a vibrant and unusual visitor from America was in the area. Lorenzo Dow, known as 'Crazy Dow'—hero of many an American Camp Meeting—was on an extended visit to England and Ireland and was preaching in the locality. He inspired these friends with colourful stories of days he had known of preaching and prayer in the camp meetings of America that had been powerfully used by God. Surely, thought Clowes and the group surrounding him, what Dow had witnessed in his own country could happen in the Potteries too. Hesitant at first, they began to lay their plans. Mow Cop, a nearby prominence rising to more than 1,000 feet above sea level, with its rocky terrain, seemed an ideal location. Perhaps they too could have a 'camp meeting' when they could preach and pray all day with no one to hinder them.

At last a date was fixed for the first English 'camp meeting'. But when 31 May 1807 dawned the weather was drizzling and overcast. Undeterred a small group of men and women climbed to the top of Mow Cop and, standing near a wall for shelter, began to sing and pray aloud. Then one of their number began to preach a sermon. Gradually as others living in the vicinity climbed the hill to join them, they decided another person should address the people. Now the numbers began to swell and a flag was hoisted to show newcomers where to gather. And still the numbers grew. Clowes himself then mounted the makeshift pulpit and told the listening crowd what God had done for him, turning his life upside down and making him a new man. Soon those who had climbed Mow Cop had multiplied to such an extent that yet another preaching station was opened, then another and another, until four men were preaching simultaneously to the ever-increasing numbers. Many were converted to God that day, while others were deeply moved by the power of the preaching they had heard. 'The camp meeting continued full of glory and converting power,' reported Clowes. The day only ended when darkness began to shroud the craggy hill and reluctantly the people returned to their homes.

So great had been the blessing on that first 'camp meeting' that people called to mind the earliest years of the great evangelical revival of the previous century when Wesley and Whitefield had preached boldly in the open air and in the market places. Another date was soon set for a similar day of preaching. But not everyone was pleased. Instead of recognizing these unusual events as a work of God, the local Methodist Society resented the ardour of the young men. They seemed to have forgotten that the elderly John Wesley had visited Burslem a year before his death and had written in his journal, '28 March 1790: At Burslem I was obliged to preach abroad such were the multitudes of the people.' The first one to be expelled from the Burslem Methodist Society for organizing camp meetings was Hugh Bourne.

Cast out

For some months Clowes hesitated about continuing their

endeavours. A young Christian, he found it hard to be cast out from the very group of believers where he had so recently found spiritual life. But two years after that first camp meeting Clowes had made up his mind. He was willing to be identified with the despised cause that God was evidently blessing. He attended a further camp meeting on 9 October 1809 and on this occasion ventured to preach his first sermon. Retribution followed swiftly. Soon afterwards he discovered that his name had been omitted from the list of Class Leaders of the Burslem Society—a position he had held for some years. On asking the reason, Clowes was told that his membership had been terminated and that he was no longer welcome to attend the services.

But God had not cast him out. On hearing that Clowes had effectually been excommunicated, an eccentric old Tunstall villager, one who had previously invited Clowes to hold weeknight gatherings in his kitchen, was so incensed that 'they have put Billy off the plan' that he invited Clowes to hold Sunday services in his home. Gradually a small group of societies was formed with Tunstall as their headquarters. A new denomination—Primitive Methodism—had been created, not willingly, but because the old bottles of traditional Methodism could no longer contain the new wine of God's evident blessing on the endeavours of a small group of friends.

It was also becoming obvious that God had given Clowes, still working as a master potter, exceptional preaching gifts. Sacrificially, several members of the new society each pledged five shillings a week to support Clowes and to free him to concentrate fully on the work of preaching and travelling. For a man who could earn as much as a pound a day this represented a considerable sacrifice, not only for William but also for Hannah. She would now face long periods on her own as William travelled the country in much the same way as John Wesley had done in the previous century.

Only an overwhelming sense of the need of the men and women to whom he preached supported William Clowes in these days. Trudging from village to village, he faced the same persecution as the early Methodists in the previous century. Hostile crowds exercised all their ingenuity to disturb his preaching. Sleepless nights in noisy inns and little to eat except crab apples gleaned as he passed by brought even the strong William Clowes to a degree of exhaustion he had never experienced before. But still he went on, and God sustained him with a remarkable sense of his love.

On one occasion Clowes wrote in his journal that when the burden of the spiritual condition of the people seemed almost crushing in its weight, he experienced 'a glorious baptism into the ministry' when 'the glory of God was revealed to me and a sweetness was imparted to my spirit it is impossible to describe.'

For eight years Clowes could be found preaching far and wide, and God owned his efforts: Cheshire, Lancashire, Derbyshire, Nottingham, Leicestershire all heard the preaching of 'Primitive Methodism's mighty evangelist'. Societies of believers were gathered together in a number of 'preaching stations', for these were days of an unusual outpouring of the Spirit of God that was taking place during the early decades of the nineteenth century.

Return to Hull

At last in 1819 William Clowes found himself once more on the road to Hull—scene of some of his early follies. And in Hull God chose to stamp his greatest blessings on the ministry of William Clowes, delighting to demonstrate his superior power over the works of darkness. As Clowes returned to the very haunts where his disgraceful behaviour had brought him shame, he recorded his feelings: 'I took a walk up and down the streets and lanes in which I had formerly wrought folly and wickedness ... Oh, what gratitude filled my soul ... I am now saved by grace and a missionary of the cross.' Here Hannah joined him and they knew once more some semblance of family life.

Hull had experienced many conversions in the recent past through the preaching of Dr Joseph Milner, and now the city was to know further days of the unusual blessing under the labours of Clowes and other Primitive Methodist preachers. As elsewhere there was violent opposition at first. Missiles of all descriptions were hurled through windows where meetings were in progress; church bells and local bands were used to drown the preacher's words. But Clowes, gifted with a penetrating voice, could not be silenced. Camp meetings were quickly established and within four months of his arrival four hundred had professed conversion and had joined different societies. These were not regular church attenders, rather they were converts from the rough society of the Hull streets and lanes—men and women rescued from the degrading effects of a godless lifestyle.

From Hull Clowes travelled to the surrounding towns and villages and then northwards until he had reached such towns as Ripon, Scarborough and Whitby. Wherever he went he preached in barn or chapel, field or moorland, and the power of God accompanied the preaching to such an extent that many were broken down with a realization of their sins and converted to God. Such converts were banded together into societies after the Methodist pattern and, whenever there were sufficient numbers to justify it, chapels were built and preachers sent out on a regular basis to teach the people. Two years after he had started work in Hull, Clowes could write of the 'many chapels built and the land spread over with many living churches, and hundreds and thousands of souls brought to God.'

With the work well established in Hull, Clowes' efforts extended to many other parts of the country during the next twenty years of his life. Troubles and hindrances there certainly were: troubles with hostile mobs, troubles with fellow workers, financial anxieties and problems with young Christians. Most subtle of all were the attacks on his own spirit from the evil one whose kingdom was being assailed on every hand. Hannah herself died in 1833 after a long and distressing illness. Through all this William Clowes persevered and the work increased, embracing far distant parts of the country in its influence. In Hull itself it was estimated that after only seven years some twelve thousand people gave every promise of true conversion and had been added to the churches.

The secret of his usefulness

Although exceptionally gifted and raised up by God for a witness to his generation, these factors alone could not account for the degree of blessing accompanying the preaching of William Clowes. On one thing all who knew him were agreed: the secret of his usefulness lay in his intense and passionate life of prayer and his unshakeable confidence in God. 'When he wanted a particular blessing,' wrote an early biographer, 'his course was diligently to examine the Scriptures, and if he found that God had promised it, he took the promise as a man would take a cheque to the bank, assured that God could not deny himself.' The foundation stone on which all his achievements were built was Christ himself. 'I have always Christ,' he declared, 'and he completely satisfies me.'

The end came in 1851 when William Clowes was almost seventy-one years of age. He had been unwell for some time, worn out by his excessive travels and privations. But as his faculties failed, the approaching glory of the City of God seemed to shine more radiantly upon him. And on 2 March he left for ever the shadows of earth and entered the brightness of the presence of the One whom he had loved and served with diligence since that first Methodist lovefeast more than forty years earlier. The reporter from the *Hull Advertiser* for 7 March 1751 estimated that some ten thousand people crowded into the expansive Spring Bank Cemetery to watch their honoured leader's body laid in the grave. Engraved on the granite obelisk that marks the site are the simple words:

HE WAS A BURNING AND A SHINING LIGHT.

Grace Bennet

The saga of the two Johns

Grace Bennet, whose hand in marriage was sought by two eminent Christian preachers at the same time, was born in 1715 and converted under the preaching of George Whitefield in 1738.

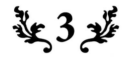

Grace Bennet

The saga of the two Johns

Attractive, graceful and vivacious, Grace Norman was always in the centre of an admiring group of friends. Her poise and skill on the dance floor earned her many an approving glance, but such adulation came at a heavy price. In later years she was to admit: 'Dancing was my darling sin and I had thereby nearly lost my life, but God was merciful and spared the sinner.'

Grace was born in Newcastle in 1715; her parents were regular in their attendance at the local parish church and the child showed early evidences of a tender conscience. Twice each Sunday the family could be found at the services and when Grace was old enough she began to read the Bible for herself. But all this was to change when her parents sent her to a dancing school shortly after her eighth birthday. Here the child quickly gained remarkable proficiency and with it the praise of all who watched her. Intoxicated with the flattery, she turned her back on the early desires she had once felt to know and please God.

Soon after her twenty-first birthday Grace married Alexander Murray, a Scotsman from a once-wealthy family which had been stripped of all its property because of its involvement with the 1715 Jacobean uprising. Alexander had, therefore, chosen a seafaring life and only four days after his marriage set sail again not to return for ten months. Grace meanwhile continued her giddy lifestyle, tempered only by the birth of her daughter shortly before Alexander's return. The call of the sea soon beckoned him once more and not until her child was over a year old did Grace receive another message from him. She learnt that he had been taken ill at sea and had returned to Portsmouth. Undertaking the long journey from Newcastle to Portsmouth, Grace was glad to find that Alexander's condition was not serious, and when he was well enough the family travelled to London.

Whitefield's influence

Here a surprise awaited them. London was ringing with stories of a young preacher named George Whitefield who had been preaching in the fields and on the common land around the town. 'Poor man,' thought Grace, 'he must be mad.' But curiosity gained the upper hand and she asked Alexander to let her go to hear him. He adamantly refused. While the family stayed in London, their young daughter was taken ill. Distressed and frantic because her child was apparently dying and had not been baptized, Grace found a book of prayers and kneeling by the baby's cot read one out earmarked 'for a departing soul'. She then offered the baby into the hands of God.

Soon after the funeral Alexander returned to sea. Depressed and lonely, Grace found little comfort in all the pleasures that had once proved so attractive to her. Her sister with whom she went to stay did all in her power to cheer her and divert Grace's mind away from her bereavement. Nothing seemed to help. At last Grace said, 'I don't know what is the matter with me, but I think it is my soul.'

'Your soul!' echoed her sister in surprise. 'You are good enough for yourself and me too.'
With Alexander far away there was nothing to prevent Grace from going to hear Whitefield preach on Blackheath Common. He was soon to return to Georgia but had been temporarily delayed, so Grace joined the crowds who flocked to listen to him. As she approached the common she could hear the singing of a mighty concourse of people, and though she had no idea of the words, the sound thrilled her with a sense of anticipation. When the preacher rose to his feet, Grace was struck by his appearance and commented, 'I thought there was something in his face I never saw in any human face before.' But his message on 'You must be born again' left her confused. Nevertheless, she returned day after day to hear the young preacher until he eventually sailed for America.

Grace had probably understood more than she realized, for shortly after this as she was reading words in the Epistle to the Romans, the light of the truth broke on her soul. With the burden of guilt removed from her conscience, Grace commented that she could now truly dance and sing as she had never done before. Soon, however, she was to face a storm of abuse. But God prepared her to withstand it by giving her a most unusual experience of his love. Describing those moments, Grace wrote:

I rejoiced with joy unspeakable … The sense of this divine manifestation the enemy could never tear away from me in all my violent temptations afterwards, even when I was almost driven to despair.

Rejection

First, her own sister, who had once delighted in Grace's lighthearted friendship, now felt acutely embarrassed by the new 'religious turn' she had taken and accused Grace of making a fool of herself. Former friends too shunned her company. But worse was to follow. Alexander was due home shortly and when he arrived Grace's sister informed him that the Methodists had affected his wife's mental balance. Alexander did not believe it, but when he discovered that Grace was unwilling to accompany him to all the places of amusement in which they had formerly delighted, his anger and distress were unmeasured. Never was any Methodist to come near his wife, nor could she attend the preaching services she loved, he insisted. Finding that he still could not drive away her new seriousness, he proclaimed her insane. 'You shall forsake those Methodists or I will put you into the mad house,' he declared, dismally adding that all his happiness in this world had been destroyed.

'I believe them to be the people of God,' replied Grace stoutly, 'and if I deny them, I should also deny the Lord who bought me with his blood. Put me in whatever place you please, the Lord will go with me.'

Alexander stormed out of the house saying, 'I am going now to book a place for you.' Grace had only one recourse in her need. She poured out her sorrows and her plight before God. Presently there was the sound of footsteps on the stairs. Alexander was back. 'I can't do it,' he said simply. Shortly afterwards Grace was taken seriously ill. Realizing he could well lose the woman he truly loved, Alexander capitulated. 'My dear, will you have anyone sent for?' he asked. Even though he left the room when any Methodist preacher came to visit Grace, Alexander had begun to soften to the message they brought. On her recovery, he allowed Grace to attend the Methodist preaching services, and before his return to the sea once more in 1741 there was evidence that he too shared her faith in Christ. It was to be Alexander's last voyage. After he had been absent for many months, Grace received a message informing her that her husband had died at sea.

Return to Newcastle
So at twenty-six years of age, the young widow returned to her mother's home in Newcastle and took work as a domestic servant in order to support herself. Sensitive by nature, Grace was plunged into a further period of depression after Alexander's death. But now there was an added dimension:

an intense spiritual conflict. Having heard many gifted preachers in London, Grace became highly critical of those to whom she now listened. Before she had been the centre of attention due to her difficult circumstances, now she felt neglected and alone. She reacted resentfully. The enemy of souls took advantage of these things, and sowed sceptical and unbelieving thoughts in her mind until a dark cloud of unbelief enveloped the young Christian. One day as she walked in a field beyond the town walls, Satan threw his last and most venomous dart. 'Perhaps it is all a lie! There is no God.'

'Satan, you are a liar,' she cried out in despair. I know there is a God. I have felt his power. I have tasted his love.' Still there was no reply from heaven, only further taunts from the enemy. Grace climbed a high flight of steps to the top of a tower on the town wall. If there were no God, then she would throw herself down to her own destruction. Nothing mattered any more. She gave one last heavenward cry. 'If there be a God, save me.' And the tempter fled. Gradually Grace came to see that she had grieved the Spirit of God by her critical and acrimonious attitudes. He had allowed these circumstances both to humble her and to prepare her for a life of eminent usefulness.

The two Johns
During 1742 John Wesley paid his first visit to Newcastle. When he saw the response of the people to his message, the Methodist leader decided to make the city the northern focus of his work and to set up an orphan home to meet the urgent needs he discovered. In the following years he paid many

visits to Newcastle and Grace Murray became one of Wesley's most valued workers. She cared for the children, tended sick preachers who came to Newcastle to rest and worked among the women. In 1748 Wesley himself was taken ill during a visit to the city. For six days Grace nursed him. Then, to her astonishment, just before he left he made her a proposal of marriage. Flattered and amazed, Grace scarcely knew what to say, but expressed her delight. To Wesley's mind her words were an assent and he regarded himself as engaged to Grace. When he was due to leave Newcastle, he expressed the hope that when they next met they would never part again. But Grace begged to be allowed to accompany him on his travels to care for him and help with the work among women in the Methodist societies. To this Wesley agreed.

The party spent some time in Yorkshire where Wesley faced hostile mobs, and was injured on several occasions. Grace stood by him courageously. Then they travelled on into Derbyshire to visit the societies where another of Wesley's preachers, John Bennet, had been working . Here a serious problem arose. The previous year John Bennet had been ill and had come to Newcastle. Grace had nursed him throughout a six-month period. A strong affection had sprung up between them and they had corresponded regularly ever since. Now they met again and all the warmth of their friendship was rekindled. Wesley, possibly unaware of the situation, decided to travel on to London on his own, leaving Grace to return to Newcastle.

Realizing that he was about to lose Grace, John Bennet wrote to Wesley requesting permission to marry her. 'Utterly amazed', Wesley replied to Bennet's letter, but presumed sadly that by the time his letter reached them they would be already married. This was not the case, however. Though natural affection dictated that Bennet was the one Grace ought to marry, a sense of privilege and a desire for the greatest usefulness in the service of God still attracted the young widow to Wesley. Neither man knew her true feelings, and nor, it seems, did she; and for six agonizing months Grace vacillated between the two Johns. Sometimes she gave one cause for hope and sometimes the other. Both men prevaricated over claiming her as his bride, now resigning her to the other, now declaring her to be his own. At last the situation appeared to clarify and in October 1749 Grace was on the verge of marrying John Wesley. Then Charles Wesley was informed of the situation. Saddling his horse, he dashed up the country, collected Grace and took her to where Bennet was staying. Perhaps he was unhappy about his brother marrying a woman with no classical education, but in the event he would not leave until he had seen John Bennet and Grace satisfactorily married. John Wesley's heart was broken.

Grace and John Wesley met only briefly afterwards and then not again for thirty-nine years. The two preachers also went their separate ways on both doctrinal and emotional grounds. Grace was thirty-four when she remarried and five sons were born to the couple in quick succession. John was responsible for a widely scattered circuit of societies. This meant long periods away from home which was far from satisfactory with his rapidly increasing family. So after four years of marriage John Bennet, who was in fact a very able preacher, became the pastor of an Independent church in Warburton, Cheshire.

Here Grace took every opportunity to serve God: she visited the sick and conducted a regular meeting for the women in her home.

Widowhood

But after only ten years of married life, Grace was widowed once more, and her boys, the eldest of whom was only eight, left without a father. With his health crumbling through excessive toil, John had also suffered a serious accident, cutting his leg badly. Infection set in and for four months Grace cared for him, struggling to save his life.

'My dear, I am dying,' said John as it became evident that his life was slipping away.

'Are you afraid?' asked Grace.

'No, no, my dear, for I am assured past a doubt that I shall be with the Lord to behold his glory. The blood of Jesus Christ has cleansed me from all sin,' replied John. Then he prayed for Grace, for his sons, for the church.

'Can you stake your soul on the doctrine you have preached?' asked Grace earnestly as she realized the end was nearing.

'Yes, even if I had ten thousand souls,' he replied and, despite his growing weakness, declared, 'Sing, sing, yes, shout for joy!' Kissing Grace for the last time, he died in her arms.

Forty-four years of widowhood lay ahead of Grace—years

of loneliness and trial, but years of proving the sufficiency of God. Prayer became her most important ministry and the throne of grace a constant refuge. She continued weekly services in her home to which her neighbours could come and listen to the preachers whom she had invited. Young people flocked to her for advice and prayer. In days when medical knowledge and help was limited and often unobtainable, the locals turned to Grace Bennet for advice. Her years of experience caring for sick preachers in Newcastle had given her much practical wisdom. Gifted in managing her domestic concerns, Grace found time to cultivate her mind and she devoted many hours to reading. Books to strengthen her in the spiritual life were a priority, but she also read and enjoyed historical records and the works of the great national poets.

At the surprising age of seventy-seven, Grace began to keep a journal, recording her daily spiritual struggles and triumphs. Marked by a refreshing honesty, her diary demonstrates the quality of this Christian woman. She did not hesitate to record her failures: 'This is a heavy day for me. I dare not connive at sin for it will find us out, be it ever so secret. Indeed, I own before God my weakness that I am of a sharp spirit.' And there were better days: 'This morning has been a good one; the Lord has been with us in family worship and comforted my soul greatly.' She hated to hear gossip and backbiting, having herself been taught so painfully by God of the results of such a spirit. 'Indeed, this is a sin we should flee from as from a serpent. I can truly say I have been pained to my heart by hearing evil speaking. I have condemned myself for not reproving it,' she wrote. She longed for more growth in grace: 'I have need of power to watch and pray, for I find enemies without and within, and my own heart the worst of all; but God is greater than my heart and on him I rely.'

In 1793, when Grace Bennet was seventy-eight, increasing infirmity made it difficult for her to walk the distance to the Warburton chapel. Her friends urged her to move back to the area where she and John had lived during the first four years of their married life—to Chapel-en-le-Frith in Derbyshire. Grace agreed, praying that God would make her new home a house of prayer. Again she gathered together small groups of believers for times of fellowship, and continued to know the comfort of God's presence in her hours alone. 'In reading Flavel on 'Providence'[1] what scenes were opened up to me in my own life!' she recorded. 'What dangers have I escaped from! What sins has the Lord by his providence preserved me from! Stand astonished, O my soul, at the loving-kindness of the Lord!' In spite of this, the sin that caused her most distress was the sin of her own lack of faith: 'O wicked damning unbelief,' she wrote vehemently as she was conscious of failing yet again. 'My soul is many times sick through this many-headed monster. When I think that it is gone, it rears its head again … It is of God's wonderful mercy that I am not cut off and cast into hell … but I have an Advocate above, a friend before the throne of love.'

Final trials

As the years passed Grace mused on the approach of that last enemy: death. 'It is easy to talk about death at a distance, but it is awful to look him in the face without an Advocate,' she wrote. The last and hardest trial of her failing years was the virtual loss of her eyesight. Now there were no more entries in her diary, for she could no longer see to write. Worst of all, she could no longer read the Scriptures for herself as she had loved to do. She tried every expedient she could to make out the words or even just the sense of the passage. And when she failed, as fail she did, scalding tears ran from her unseeing eyes on to the open pages in front of her.

At eighty-eight years of age Grace Bennet came to the end of her journey. Although she could no longer read, she could pray, and as she sat in her room, frail and almost blind, her mind ran to her Christian friends from long ago and she would pray for them; she would pray for the blessing of God upon his church and for herself that God would give her added grace for the trial that lay ahead. To the end she faced the fierce assaults of the tempter, but her Saviour came to help her through the last deep river. 'When will his chariot wheels advance to call his exile home? Sweet Jesus, come quickly! My soul is at rest,' were among her last words. And on 23 February 1803 those chariots of God carried Grace Bennet home.

Note

1   Flavel, J., *The Mystery of Providence*, London, Banner of Truth Trust, 1963.

4

Thomas Lee

'A good soldier of Jesus Christ'

Tommy Lee can be ranked among the most courageous of the early Methodist preachers of the eighteenth-century Evangelical Revival. He itinerated first of all in Yorkshire under the direction of William Grimshaw and later in many far flung parts of the country.

4

Thomas Lee

'A good soldier of Jesus Christ'

'We have done enough to make an end of him,' cried a voice as stones, clods of earth and other missiles rained down on the young Methodist preacher. This was Thomas Lee's first experience of that mindless brutality so often the lot of the itinerant preachers in the early days of the eighteenth-century revival. Undaunted by the pain, Tommy Lee afterwards declared, 'I never found my soul more happy nor was ever more composed in my closet.' 'But,' he admitted, 'I did indeed reel to and fro, and my head was broken by a stone.'

Born in Keighley, Yorkshire, in 1727, Thomas had lost his

mother at the age of four and was subsequently brought
up in his uncle's home in Addingham, seven miles north of
Keighley. A good home, it stood in marked contrast to the
decadence and vice which characterized much of the country
in those days before the revival had transformed homes and
society itself. Tommy was 'carefully restrained from outward
sin' by his uncle and aunt. A naturally serious boy, he could
later recognize God's overruling in the circumstances of his
childhood and realized that God had frequently been working
in him from his early years. The thought of hell and eternal
punishment often filled the boy with panic, but in spite of
his dread of such a destiny, the alternative set before him of
loving and pleasing God seemed a dull and unattractive one.
Yet even from the age of ten or eleven the words 'eternity'
and 'everlasting' troubled him so much that the thought of
annihilation after death seemed a preferable option. There was
no gospel preaching in that area of Yorkshire to enlighten the
boy's mind or to bring peace to his disturbed conscience.

At the age of fourteen Tommy was apprenticed to the
worsted trade—an industry for which the area was noted.
Once more he was placed with a kindly family and lived in a
situation suited to his serious turn of mind. He began to read
the Bible in his spare moments and even found delight in
secret prayer. But as he grew to manhood these early religious
impressions began to fade. Impatiently he tried to shake them
off completely, aiming to find his pleasure in the light-hearted
society of his contemporaries instead. But try as he might, he
seemed to find little satisfaction in the company he had now
chosen; in fact he experienced a lingering sense of shame as

he associated with young people whose conversation and way of life was both blasphemous and unwholesome.

A new work

At this very time a new work of God was beginning to unfold in eighteenth-century Yorkshire. During Tommy Lee's teenage years the preaching of Benjamin Ingham and others was gradually penetrating even the country districts, where Tommy lived, radiating outwards from Ingham's home town of Ossett, south of Leeds. John Nelson, a stonemason from Birstall, was another who spent every spare moment in itinerant preaching around his home. And even more notably, from 1742 onwards, the passionate preaching of William Grimshaw in Haworth, a Pennine village only ten miles south of Addingham, was affecting the entire area. To set his troubled conscience at rest Tommy would occasionally join the crowds who flocked each Sunday to Haworth. There the teenager listened to 'that blessed man of God, Mr Grimshaw', as he would one day call him, though certainly that time had not yet come. Stirred but not converted, Tommy Lee made noble resolutions to improve himself, but without the power of the inner life of God in his soul, he soon relapsed into his former ways.

Tommy Lee's eventual conversion was not a dramatic affair; instead it came in the form of a gradual understanding as he listened more and more frequently to the Methodist lay preachers, whose journeys brought them ever nearer to Tommy's home. Heroic men they were, men such as Paul Greenwood and Jonathan Maskew, who sometimes scarcely escaped with their lives from the vicious mobs who assailed them. Gradually Tommy began to find the Bible to be his increasing and constant delight, while the company of such men as Greenwood and Maskew seemed to him the most finest on earth. At last he decided to drop his former companions and cast in his lot with these 'despised Methodists'. And as he later wrote, 'Blessed be God, from that hour I never had one desire to turn back.'

Although in all likelihood Tommy was indeed truly converted at this time he lacked any inner assurance of his acceptance with God. Instead the young man remained tossed about spiritually for more than a year. Scarcely twenty-four hours would pass without some fierce spiritual conflict distressing him as he constantly found himself torn between doubt and hope. So great was his fear at times in case he would be rejected by God at the last day, that he pledged in his heart that he would never count any suffering, affliction or sorrow too heavy to be endured if only he could receive that inner assurance of God's love and acceptance he so earnestly longed to know. And so Tommy struggled on day after day, sometimes lifted up with fresh confidence, only to be dashed with renewed uncertainties. But God had not forgotten him and one day, as he was at his regular employment, a strange impulse gripped his mind suggesting to him that at that very moment God was willing to hear him pray. He later described the moments that followed:

I left my business immediately and went to prayer. In a moment God broke in upon my soul in so wonderful a manner, that I could no longer doubt of his forgiving love. I cried, 'My

Lord and my God!' And in the spirit I was then in, I could have praised and loved and waited to all eternity.

The young evangelist

Assured at last of his salvation nothing could now hold Tommy Lee back from speaking freely to his friends and neighbours of their own need of a Saviour. Encouraged by their response to his initial efforts, he began to venture further afield. All day he worked at his business and each evening set off to one of the numerous villages dotted across the desolate moors surrounding his home, areas such as Ilkley Moor and Rombalds Moor, where few messengers of Jesus Christ had yet ventured. Everywhere he went God used the words of the fiery young evangelist to alarm and convert those to whom he spoke.

Sometimes Lee, still scarcely more than twenty years of age, would wonder whether it was God's will that he should be speaking to others in this way at all. Had God really called him to preach? Then he would confide his fears to William Grimshaw, whose own zeal and energy as a gospel preacher had become a pattern that Tommy earnestly tried to copy. No one gave him more encouragement or took greater delight in the ardour of this young man than the curate of Haworth. 'Go on,' he would urge, 'and be valiant in the work to which God has called you.'

Such reassurance was well timed, for it was not long before Tommy Lee was called upon to face a baptism of suffering—a baptism common to many of the early lay preachers at that time but one which would have silenced a more timid spirit for ever. At Pateley Bridge, some ten miles north of his home, Lee encountered for the first time a brutal and mindless attack from a mob maddened by hatred and inflamed by liquor. Incited by the local vicar, who doubtless resented the presence of the young preacher in his parish, the loutish rabble began to hurl mud, stones and any other missile which was to hand at Tommy.

Reeling to and fro with the blood pouring from the wound on his head, he later confessed that he experienced an inner calm sweeter even than the joy he knew while praying to God alone in his room. Such suffering was not without purpose for several dated their conversion from that very occasion. Undaunted by the pain, Tommy proceeded to the next town as soon as his wound was cleaned and bandaged, and began once more to preach to the gathered crowd. Some of the mob from Pateley Bridge had followed him, but without the stimulus of the vicar's incitements they were outnumbered and silent.

Grimshaw's advice

Not long after this Tommy Lee married Mary, a young woman who shared both his faith and his sacrificial zeal. During the following four years he continued his secular employment in order to support her, preaching during the day and then working through the night. But gradually, even though he was still in his twenties, his health began to break down under the strain. Unwilling to reduce his strenuous programme of preaching, Lee again found his way to Haworth where he consulted Grimshaw, his kindly friend and adviser.

Grimshaw was in no doubt as to what the young man should do. He must sell his business, buy a horse and give himself unreservedly to the work of proclaiming the gospel. How could he support himself and Mary? Tommy wondered. And Grimshaw was ready with an answer. His income would be meagre, but his support would come from the grateful men and women whose lives had been transformed through his preaching. To stimulate him to yet greater endeavour in the service of his Master, Grimshaw wrote:

> I hope your bow abides in strength and that you can preach twenty times a week. If you can preach oftener, do. Preaching is health, food and physic [medicine) to me, and why not to thee, my brother. Besides, Tommy, there is very great need of preaching now, for iniquity aboundeth, the love of many grows cold and God's judgements are out in the earth. Tommy, let us preach four times a day or thirty times a week, whichever you please or can better bear. Our Master well deserves it. Yea, and infinitely more. Oh, that we may spend and be spent in preaching his everlasting gospel, in converting sinners and confirming believers.

The high cost

With such an example before him, Tommy Lee determined to preach with yet more dedication. But the cost was high. All he had suffered at Pateley Bridge was little compared with the cup of pain and indignity yet reserved for this earnest ambassador of Jesus Christ. 1752 had been a year of exceptional progress for the work of God in that area, and young Tommy Lee knew that to disturb the kingdom of Satan in the way he was doing was to invite vicious reprisals.

As he and his wife Mary rode once more through Pateley Bridge, the mob spotted the preacher they had previously assaulted. Closing in on their prey, they pulled Lee from his horse, and as he lay on the ground helpless, repeatedly struck him against the stones. Was he still alive? Not content with such brutality, they hauled him by his hair to a nearby house and threw him against the stone steps, injuring his back so severely that he could not walk without pain for many years to come. Even this was not enough. Next his tormentors dragged the injured man to the sewer which carried the effluence from the town to the river. Rolling him in the muck, they then threw him into the river, doubtless anticipating that his injuries would make it impossible for him to climb out. But slowly and painfully, Tommy inched his way back on to the bank and lay there exhausted.

At that moment his wife, Mary, who had been a horrified and helpless spectator of such brutality, crossed over to him and tried to help him. 'What! Are you a Methodist?' cried a coarse voice behind her. Several blows in the mouth sent her reeling backwards, bleeding. Some suggested throwing her in the river also, while others thought it would be better to kill Tommy outright. Disagreeing on the matter, these thugs suddenly noticed that others had gathered to see what was happening. Leaving Tommy and his wife, the gang rushed off to try and throw these unwelcome spectators into the river as well.

Alone at last with her injured husband, Mary succeeded in dragging Tommy to the place where his horse had been grazing. As he began to recover a little strength, she managed to help him up on to his horse and then led the animal gently to the home of a friend. Here Tommy was bathed, given a change of clothes and his wounds dressed. After resting for a short while, he determined to ride on to a nearby village where he knew eager people were waiting to hear him preach. He addressed the expectant crowd using the verse of Scripture: 'Many are the afflictions of the righteous, but the Lord delivers him out of them all'. His bruised and battered body provided all the illustration needed for such a message.

Undeterred

The next day, undeterred by the stabbing pains in his back and his aching limbs, Lee rode along the back roads to a nearby area known as North Pasture. Here a crowd of serious listeners, no doubt aware of the reprehensible acts perpetrated the previous day, gathered to hear him preach. The ringleader of the mob responsible for the brutal attack lurked around. He could do no more, however, than disturb the worship by breaking every pane of glass in the house where the people had gathered. But God was present to restrain the evil and pour out his blessing. Many wept as they listened; others rejoiced in the privilege of suffering for Christ's sake. Tommy Lee returned to his home, peaceful and glad, but too sore and bruised even to undress himself without help.

This was not the end of his troubles. Unwilling to leave the converts in the Pateley Bridge area without ministry and encouragement, Lee ventured again and again into this hostile territory. Each time it was the same. For a while all would be peaceful, then the mob, ever vigilant for an opportunity to destroy this messenger of Jesus Christ would break in to the house where he was preaching and try to snatch him. On one occasion Lee was forced to leap from an upstairs window into the arms of waiting friends in order to outwit his persecutors.

Gradually he became wiser to their ways, and when they determined once again to throw him into the River Nidd, then in full flood, he laid hold on his assailant with so tenacious a grip that if one fell into the water, the other would share the unwelcome experience. On another occasion the mob heard that Lee was due to preach on the far side of the river. Dividing their forces, they set off to guard all the bridges where he might be intending to cross. This meant that Lee and his small band were forced to ride many miles out of their way to avoid the gangs. On that dark winter's night they soon lost their way on the moors. Drenched by rain and snow, they wandered along the moorland tracks for over two hours until at last they found the home where the agitated congregation was waiting, fearful that their brave preacher might have been attacked or even killed. Changing from his sodden clothes, Lee preached to them even though the hour was late. And God was unusually present with his people. 'It seemed to us little less than heaven,' commented Lee. 'It was a blessed day to my soul.'

But even so courageous a man as Tommy Lee sometimes fainted under the burden of his sufferings:

I remember once, during these seasons of trouble, a thought came into my mind, 'It is hard to have no respite, to be thus perpetually suffering.' Immediately it was impressed upon my mind, 'Did you not, when you were on the borders of despair, promise the Lord, that if he would give you an assurance of his favour, you would count no suffering, sorrow or affliction too great to be endured for his name's sake?' This at once silenced all murmuring, and thenceforth I bore whatever befell me with patience and after with joy, finding a willingness to bear it, as long as he saw meet, if it were to the end of my life.

Wider usefulness

William Grimshaw, himself no stranger to persecution at the hands of a mob incited by some antagonistic cleric, could not help but love Tommy Lee, finding in him a kindred spirit to his own. Writing to John Wesley, he recommended the young preacher for wider usefulness, although this would inevitably mean that he would lose Lee's assistance in the Great Haworth Round, as Grimshaw's own preaching circuit had become known. Manfully Grimshaw agreed to shoulder the extra responsibility in order to free his young friend to go wherever Wesley might send him. From 1758 until his death nearly thirty years later, Lee was to be found preaching in far distant parts of the land: Newcastle, Edinburgh, Lincolnshire, Derbyshire, and many other places as well.

But moving from the area of Pateley Bridge did not herald the end of the sufferings of this valiant soldier of Jesus Christ. At Newark-on-Trent eggs filled with blood and painted with tar were hurled at him. Here again he was dragged from his horse, thrown in a ditch and then bedaubed with paint. Such injuries as Tommy Lee had sustained in the work of the gospel told on his health, and well before his sixtieth birthday his strength began to fail.

Far from grieving over the trials he had endured, however, this courageous preacher described his sufferings in these words:

> If I, at this moment, saw all the sufferings I have had for his [Christ's] name's sake, if they were now spread before me, I would say, 'Lord, if thou wilt give me strength, I will now begin again, and thou shalt add to them lions' dens, and fiery furnaces, and by thy grace I will go through them all.' My life, though attended with many crosses, has been a life of mercies.

Lovely Jerusalem

Preaching on the Sunday before he died in 1786, Thomas Lee was leaning painfully on crutches. An inflammation in one foot, probably from some injury sustained in mob violence, had spread rapidly up the leg, and Lee himself must have realized that the end was near. He preached twice that day, basing his first sermon on the words: 'All flesh is grass', and the second on 'Surely I know it shall be well with them that fear the Lord.' Leaning forward in his pulpit, Tommy Lee declared, 'Perhaps this will be my last sermon', and then he unexpectedly announced a hymn usually reserved for funerals. As he sang the words, the prospect of the heavenly city, that everlasting refuge awaiting the people of God, moved him profoundly:

> By faith we already behold
> That lovely Jerusalem here ...

A night or two later, as the pain and infection increased, Tommy smiled for the last time at his devoted wife, Mary, and gently closed his eyes on the scene of all his earthly conflicts, to open them again in that 'lovely Jerusalem', beyond the range of insult, cruelty and torment forever. When John Wesley, himself a veteran of eighty-five years, heard of the death of his fellow worker, he spoke sadly of the loss of this valiant and indomitable preacher, describing Tommy Lee as 'a good, old soldier of Jesus Christ'.

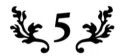

Joan Waste and William Hunter

Not counting the cost

*Joan Waste and William Hunter were two young people,
living during the same period of the sixteenth century, though
unknown to each other. Their short lives, marked by heroism
and obedience to the Word of God, deserve to be remembered
by all who value our Christian heritage.*

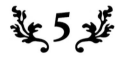

Joan Waste and William Hunter

Not counting the cost

Joan Waste

William Waste and his wife looked forward to the birth of their twins with both anticipation and some anxiety. Childbirth in the sixteenth century was fraught with hazards—the birth of twins even more so. At last the babies were safely delivered and named Roger and Joan. But the joy of the parents was tinged with sadness. As the weeks passed they realized that little Joan was quite blind.

The family lived in Derby in the English Midlands and William Waste was a barber by trade. To augment his small income he would also make ropes, dexterously twisting the strands together to produce the strength required. The twins were born in 1533 during the reign of Henry VIII—days when anyone who was not prepared to accept the religious norms imposed by a decadent church could face persecution or even death.

Only three years after the birth of the twins, far off at Vilvorde, near Antwerp, William Tyndale was being tied to a stake—martyred for having translated the Scriptures into English so that ordinary people like William Waste and his family could read them for themselves. 'Lord, open the King of England's eyes' had been Tyndale's dying prayer—a prayer that was to be remarkably answered, for not many months later the king was persuaded to allow the free circulation of the Scriptures in English.

As Joan, their blind child, grew she would help her parents in any way she could. Despite her disability she learnt to knit stockings, turning the heels with remarkable skill. By the time she reached her teenage years she was able to help her father in making ropes, her nimble fingers were rarely still. In 1547, when the twins were fourteen, Henry VIII died and his nine-year- old son, Edward, came to the throne. What sort of king would the boy become? Would the country now be released from the tortuous cycle of persecutions and martyrdoms of his father's reign?

With relief the family learnt of the easing of religious restrictions. Now they could attend their local parish church and even hear the Scriptures read in English. When

Archbishop Cranmer published his *Book of Homilies* that same year, it meant that from the pulpits of England there were to be explanations and applications of the Scripture to accompany the public reading. Joan loved to attend the daily services at All Saints Parish Church in Derby. Blind though she was, she could listen carefully and soon began to understand the truths of Scripture. Her mind and heart opened to the gospel of redemption through the sacrifice of Christ with the Bible becoming precious above all things to the girl.

Her New Testament

If only she could possess a copy for her very own, thought Joan, even though she had never been taught to read because her blindness made such a skill unnecessary. Despite this she longed above everything else to own a copy of the New Testament. Every penny she could earn as she helped her father twisting the ropes was carefully saved until at last the day came when Joan had managed to save a sum sufficient to purchase a coveted New Testament. But who could read it to her? Then she remembered a poor old man of seventy, John Hurt, who had been thrown into the debtors' prison in Derby for some trifling offence. She knew he could read, and with time on his hands he might well help her.

And John Hurt was very willing to read the words to Joan even though she would sometimes interrupt him and ask him to read a passage again and again. An intelligent girl, she learnt long passages of Scripture by heart so that she could recall them as she sat twisting ropes or helping her parents in other ways. When the old prisoner was ill or could not read to her, Joan would find someone else to do so. Not everyone was as obliging as John Hurt, and if no one would read to her free of charge, Joan would pay from her earnings for the service. Not to be cheated, she would stipulate exactly how many chapters should be read for each penny, and how many times over certain chapters should be repeated before her reader was paid.

Then came two great changes in Joan Waste's life. While she was still a teenager her parents died. Dependent on their care, Joan may have wondered what she would do now, but her twin brother, Roger, undertook to provide for his sister. The second change was the death of the boy king, Edward VI, at only sixteen years of age. His reign had ushered in an unprecedented period of prosperity for the Christian church. The boy's dying prayer: 'O Lord God, save thy chosen people of England. O my Lord God, defend this realm from papistry and maintain the true religion' must have touched many a heart. It also came as a warning of trials that might lie ahead.

Trial of faith

In 1553 Mary, Edward's bigoted Catholic half-sister, came to the throne. Many in the church had only adopted Protestant principles for the sake of an easy life. Now these clerics gladly reverted to their former ways. But Joan Waste remained firm to her convictions and clung steadfastly to her faith. By now the long portions of Scripture that Joan had learnt had given her a strong inner resource—an unshakeable persuasion, coupled with the ability to demonstrate succinctly the clear doctrines of the Reformation. This was not mere head knowledge, for all who knew Joan spoke also of her attractive

Christian character and her zeal for the souls of others. It grieved the young woman deeply to hear those whose opinions she had formerly respected now openly denying the very truths she had learnt from their lips. Her conscience would now no longer allow her to attend services of worship when the truths of the gospel on which her salvation depended were being openly rejected from the pulpit.

Joan knew well the likely consequences of such a course of action and she had not long to wait. 1555 was to prove one of the darkest years in the history of the English church, as the new queen's ruthless determination to bring her country back to the Church of Rome rekindled the fires of persecution throughout the land. Joan's fearless stand for truth soon came to the attention of the church dignitaries. That summer Joan was arraigned to appear before a local tribunal made up of Ralph Baynes, Bishop of Lichfield and Coventry, and others. Proceedings began with the vicious and familiar interrogation, well known from the previous reign. Did she believe that in the sacrament of the Mass the elements of bread and wine were changed into the actual body and blood of the Saviour?

'I believe what I have been taught both from the Scriptures and from what I have learnt from the pulpit of this church,' replied the blind girl courageously, knowing only too well the cost of such an answer. Twisting the argument against her accusers, Joan asked them whether in the Day of Judgement they would be prepared to bear upon their consciences the burden of having taught the people anything contrary to the Scriptures. If they could not, why did they not leave a poor blind girl alone? Unable to give a straight answer to such a pertinent question the bishop merely demanded to know whether or not she would recant of her 'heretical notions'.

If her inquisitors were not prepared to accept responsibility for the teaching they were giving, then, replied Joan, neither would she give them an answer to their question. But the girl stood no chance against these biased and unjust men who would certainly not wish to be shown up by an uneducated blind woman. Without further ado Joan Waste was declared to be a heretic and handed over to the bailiffs of Derby to be kept in prison until preparations for her death at the stake could be put in place. During the weeks which followed she was occasionally taken back to court as further attempts were made to force her to deny the truths she believed; sometimes her accusers visited her in prison, but never could they undermine her resolve.

Sentence of death

After five weeks Joan learnt that the sentence of death was to be carried out. We may only guess at her thoughts. Unable to write, she could leave no succinct statement of her trial nor of her unswerving faith that Christ would strengthen her to endure in her hour of need. We only know that on 1 August 1555, the young woman was eventually led to the parish church—that church so familiar to her—to hear one last sermon. That sermon was not designed to strengthen her for the suffering she must endure. Rather it was a tirade from the lips of the Chancellor, Dr Draicott, declaring that for the heresy of rejecting the Catholic teaching of the Mass, Joan Waste must perish—her body in the fire and her soul in hell.

One person, at great personal risk, stood by Joan in her extremity. It was Roger her twin brother. He took his blind sister gently by the hand and led her out of the town, accompanied by the crowd of onlookers, some hostile, some sorrowing, to the place known as Windmill Pit. Here a pyre had been built. Before the cruel flames were lit, Joan begged the prayers of the people; and she herself cried to the Saviour to have mercy on her soul and to support her to the last.

The death of a blind woman, only twenty-two years of age, might count little in the esteem of her persecutors, but in the eyes of God the Judge of all it was infinitely precious. Joan was just one of many prepared to face a fiery death rather than deny the truths of God's Word on which all their hopes for heaven had been pinned. In that same dark year of 1555 some of England's finest citizens could be numbered among that vast and still growing number of those who have been 'faithful until death'. John Rogers, who had completed Tyndale's unfinished translation of the Scriptures, was among them; so was John Bradford, Hugh Latimer and Nicholas Ridley. Such names are well known, but names such as that of Joan Waste should not be forgotten.

William Hunter

William Hunter deserves a place among many others whose brave stand for truth should not be forgotten. An Essex boy of only nineteen years of age, his steadfast testimony marks him out as one of the most courageous young people of all time. William was born in 1535, two years after Joan Waste, and in his Brentwood home he and his brother, Robert were privileged to have the truths of Scripture diligently taught to them from their earliest days. William's father may well have purchased one of the copies of Tyndale's New Testament smuggled into the country and circulating secretly before 1536, the year when the king had at last given permission for it to be freely available in the English tongue. We do know, however, that while he was still young William Hunter responded personally to the truths he had been taught.

Soon after his sixteenth birthday the youth left his sheltered home in Brentwood to be apprenticed to a City of London silk merchant. At first all went well and William was treated favourably by his master, but in 1553, with the death of young Edward VI, everything was to change. Like Joan, William discovered that those privileges which he had enjoyed from childhood were now suddenly withdrawn. Scarcely had Mary ascended the throne before the young apprentice was told that all living within the City of London had been ordered by the parish priest to attend the sacrament of the Mass. The boy refused. His master did all in his power to force his apprentice to comply, not necessarily out of any convictions of his own, but out of fear that his business could suffer if the vindictive Bishop of London, Edmund Bonner, should hear about the stubborn apprentice. When William still refused to attend Mass, he was hastily dismissed from his post. Returning to his Brentwood home, the boy remained with his parents for some weeks.

'Meddling with the Scriptures'
Not long afterwards William happened to be passing a church

near his home. Noticing that the door was ajar, he slipped into the gloomy depths, and there to his delight, he saw an open Bible on the lectern. Alone in the church, the youth began to read aloud some of the passages of Scripture that he loved. Perhaps he did not hear approaching footsteps. When he glanced up there was the sneering face of an old man known colloquially as Father Atwell looking over his shoulder. 'How dare you meddle with the Scriptures?' snarled Atwell. 'Do you think you are able to understand them and expound them?'

'Oh no, replied William hastily, 'I was only reading for my own comfort. I would never presume to expound them.'

'The land has never been merry since we have had the Bible in English,' continued the old man.

'Oh, Father Atwell, you mustn't say that,' protested William. 'It is God's book, where we learn both what pleases and what displeases him.'

This was too much for Atwell. Cunningly he led the boy on, and by denying some of the basic truths of Scripture that meant so much to William, he trapped the boy into expressing his own strongly held convictions. 'You must turn another leaf or else you, and a great many more heretics, will broil for this,' threatened the disgruntled old man.

'God give me grace that I may believe his Word and confess his name whatever happens to me,' responded William.

Furious at the youth's gallant spirit, old Atwell stormed out of the church and into the nearby tavern where he found the vicar, Thomas Wood, drinking his pint of ale. Retelling his story of the audacious boy who dared to argue his case with him, Atwell conducted the vicar across to the church where William was still engrossed in reading the Bible. Angrily the vicar accosted William in much the same way as Atwell had done, accusing him of taking upon himself privileges reserved for the clergy. 'I will read the Scriptures while I live, and you, Master Vicar, ought not to discourage anyone from it, but ought rather to exhort people diligently to do so,' William declared.

As Atwell had done, the vicar skilfully steered the conversation round until he posed the most important question of all—from his perspective. In what way did William Hunter understand Christ's words in John 6 where he spoke of himself as the Bread of Life and of his people eating and drinking of him for salvation? The trap was set, and probably William knew it. 'Such words are to be interpreted spiritually,' William replied, 'for Christ himself said, "The words that I speak unto you, they are spirit, and they are life."' That was enough. Now Thomas Wood had incriminating evidence that the boy in front of him was, as he supposed, a heretic, and as a heretic he would be hunted down. William left the vicar with a final challenge—a challenge that was too much for him. 'If you and I were both chained to a stake for our beliefs, who would be the first to recant?' The answer was self-evident.

Pursuit and discovery

William realized that he was now in serious trouble. He

must escape immediately lest his parents should also suffer. Not many hours had passed before the local Justice and the constable were hammering on the door of the Hunter's home. 'Where is your son?' was the rough demand. When William's father protested that he did not know where his boy was, Justice Brown began to threaten him. 'Go and find him immediately, or I will have you clapped into prison as well.'

'Sir, will you have me seek out my son to be burned?' asked the distraught father. At last William's father saw he had no alternative. He must obey. So he set out from home, ostensibly looking for William, but all the time hoping earnestly that he would not find him. For three days he tramped the roads. Then he saw the boy. Weeping bitterly, his father told William all that had happened. 'I will return and say I can't find you,' said the unhappy man.

'No, father,' replied William, 'I will go home with you.' And so he did. As soon as news reached Justice Brown that the youth had been discovered, he arrived with the constable at the Hunter's home.

Without further ado William was arrested, taken to the common prison where his arms and legs were thrust into the stocks. There he remained to await further questioning.

'I hear you are a Scripture man and can reason much from the sixth of John,' was Justice Brown's opening gambit the next day.

'The vicar urged me to say what I did,' said William in defence.

One scripture after another was quoted at William to demonstrate the Catholic doctrine of the Mass. For each the boy had an answer. At last Justice Brown angrily threw down the Bible he had been holding and exclaimed, 'You naughty boy! You just explain Scripture however you wish.'

'I don't mean to, sir,' replied William respectfully, 'I earnestly want to know the mind of Christ in instituting the sacraments.'

'You are a villain indeed,' shouted Brown, his anger raised to such a pitch that no further discussion was possible. When William suggested that it would be better if they spoke again when his fury had abated, Brown replied, 'Indeed, I shall send you tomorrow to the Bishop of London and he shall examine you.' William and his parents well knew that this was virtually a death sentence. Few survived Bishop Edmund Bonner's prejudiced interrogations.

Having discovered the strength of William's convictions, Bonner, tried to undermine the youth's resolve, first with bribery, then with starvation and finally by torture. Five times Bonner brought the nineteen-year-old out for cross-questioning, hoping no doubt that he could persuade so young a man to change his mind. Nothing availed. After nine months imprisonment William was sent back to Brentwood to die.

A crown of joy

Once again he was able to see his parents. Far from trying to dissuade him, or from saving their son from the stake, William's father prayed earnestly that his son might be given courage to hold on steadfastly to the end. His mother shared the same spirit, declaring that she was proud and happy to have borne such a son who was prepared to lose his life for Christ's sake. 'Mother,' answered William, 'the little pain I shall suffer will be but short. Christ has promised me a crown of joy.' With tears of joy and sorrow the three knelt together and prayed for one another that they might all be given courage and grace for the coming trial.

The sheriff whose task it was to oversee the execution might well have been amazed when he saw his own son daring to approach William as he approached the stake, embracing him and urging him not to fear. 'I thank God I am not afraid,' replied the young martyr, 'for I have already counted the cost.' With many tears the two boys, who had perhaps played together as children, parted.

'God be with you, son William,' said his father.

'God be with you, good father,' replied the son, 'and be of good cheer for I hope we shall meet again when we shall be merry.'

William's own brother, Robert, supported him and stood with him to the last—an act that almost cost him his own life.

Still clasping a copy of the New Testament which had been

his guide throughout his short life, William Hunter was chained to the stake. As the fires were lit, cruel voices taunted him through the smoke: 'Look how you burn here, soon you will burn in hell.' But one voice shouted something else. 'William,' called his brother, Robert, 'think on the passion of Christ and be not afraid.'

'I am not afraid,' called back William as he tossed his precious Bible to his brother for his safe keeping. Lifting his arms heavenward the nineteen-year-old martyr cried out, 'Lord, Lord, Lord, receive my spirit.'

Only a blind girl of twenty-two and an apprentice boy of nineteen, but such was the love of these young people for the truths of God's Word that 'they counted not their own lives dear to themselves'.

❧ 6 ❧

John Vanderkemp

Subdued by God

The power of God to transform a man's life is remarkably demonstrated in the story of John Vanderkemp. Born in Rotterdam in 1747, Vanderkemp would ultimately become one of the earliest missionaries to South Africa serving with the London Missionary Society.

🍃 6 🍃

John Vanderkemp

Subdued by God

Born in Rotterdam in 1747, John Vanderkemp (the Anglicized rendering of Johannes Van der Kemp) was outstandingly intelligent As a schoolboy he had mastered sixteen European languages before going to Leyden University to study medicine. But in spite of this the Dutch schoolboy was a disappointment to his parents. The problem lay not in any indolence on John's part, nor even in a lack of respect for his parents. Instead it sprang from the boy's total rejection of the faith and moral standards which he had been taught from earliest days.

Tall, good-looking and bubbling with life, the young medical student had a great weakness for any pretty girl who happened to cross his path. More that this he was also an easy dupe of any one who tried to use her female charms to beguile him. Coupled with his immoral lifestyle, John had rejected the Christian faith taught in his home but still had the audacity to apply for full membership of the Dutch Reformed Church. Little wonder then that his parents grieved over him. When his older brother, also studying at Leyden University was awarded a professorship, John's wounded pride was so great that he could not bear to be seen as the less able of the two. He promptly gave up his medical career and joined the army.

At twenty-five John Vanderkemp started a relationship with a young married woman. Writing long afterwards he confessed, 'I stole her from her husband and took her to Leyden where I lived publicly with her.' But John was not without pangs of conscience, and was particularly aware of the grief he had brought to his own parents. An entry in his manuscript account of his early days is blotted with tears as he records this incident as he adds that in his view, the pain he had caused hastened his father's early death. In a desperate attempt to make amends for what he had done he sent the young woman away, but after his father's death he received her back into his home once more. Soon a daughter was born whom they named Johanna.

The child's birth gave Vanderkemp an even deeper sense of guilt. For no fault of her own this girl would have to go through life under the shadow of her parents' wrongdoing. After mutual discussion, John decided to separate from his mistress, at least until the death of her rightful husband.

Johanna was to remain with him and he would care for her as best he could.

'O when wilt thou come to me?'

Although he had long since given up any regular church attendance, for Johanna's sake he still attended occasionally. On one such occasion he heard a sermon on the text: 'O when wilt thou come to me?' (Psalm 101:2) The message was soon forgotten, but those words of Scripture awakened a nameless longing in the dissolute army officer, a desire he could not quite erase day or night however dark and unworthy his conduct became.

The eighteenth-century equivalent of night clubs proved an irresistible magnet for Vanderkemp. There he continued to contract many illicit relationships which marred his life. But one day he noticed a simply dressed country girl passing his front door. Had he seen her before? He was not sure, but any girl was of interest to him. Hurrying out, the dashing army officer introduced himself. Glad enough for someone to show interest in her, Christina told John of her unhappy home where her stepmother made her life unbearable. With typical largesse and impetuosity, John arranged alternative accommodation for the twenty-three-year old, and even began to talk to her of marriage. Here he had a surprise coming to him, for Christina was not like the flighty girls John usually met. 'I will only marry you,' she insisted, 'if you first repent of your sins, then gain my father's permission.' Christina also laid it down that Johanna, who was now seven, must be happy to accept her as a stepmother.

To forsake the Leyden dance halls was no easy matter for John Vanderkemp and he found that many of the women with whom he had previously associated now used every tactic they knew to wreak revenge on him for his neglect of them. After his marriage to Christina he decided to relinquish his commission in the army and take a long honeymoon, travelling to England with his new young wife and his daughter. But what could he do now? At last he decided to return to the medical career he had abandoned so many years ago. Edinburgh appealed to him and here he applied for and gained a place to complete his studies. While other students walked around The Meadows (parkland well-loved by Edinburgh students) discussing their intellectual problems, Vanderkemp, with a love of solitude, often climbed up to Arthur's Seat above the city. From that rocky vantage point he could gaze on the wide vistas from the Pentland Hills to the sea, with the stern castle dominating the city. But instead of such a magnificent panorama turning his mind to the God of creation about whom he had learnt in his childhood, his thoughts strayed instead even further from the truth into a maze of Greek philosophical notions and pantheistic concepts.

Searching questions

After two years of study in Edinburgh, the Dutchman passed all his examinations, returned to Holland with Christina and Johanna, settling in Middelburg, where he began his medical practice. Christina was anxious to become a church member and asked John some searching questions about Christian doctrine—questions that forced him to turn his mind back to thoughts he had long since spurned. He felt too a responsibility for Johanna's religious education. She was now ten years old; did he really wish her to be influenced by all his own sceptical ideas? Dutifully John began to instruct her from the Scriptures, but the more he studied the claims of the Son of God the more unbelieving he became. His greatest dilemma lay in the astonishing assertions made by the carpenter from Galilee who insisted that he and God the Father were one? Impossible! thought Vanderkemp with his rationalistic mindset. How could he accept accounts of Christ's miraculous intervention in the course of nature: stilling a storm, reversing lifelong deformities, even raising the dead? He couldn't. Again and again he took up his pen to write his resignation from church membership; but what effect would that have on Christina and Johanna? To make things worse Christina seemed quite unaware of her husband's inner conflicts and would constantly turn to him for answers to her many questions.

Facing a spiritual crossroad, Vanderkemp resolved to live a life of virtue as noble and upright as that attained by any Christian. He failed, not once but many times over. His sins cried out for punishment, yet if he accepted the forgiveness offered in the gospel, he felt he would only make it an excuse for more sinning. 'O when wilt thou come to me?' The words of that text from so long ago still echoed and re-echoed in his mind. At last John began to pray. 'Oh, chastise me as long and as heavily as may be necessary to make sin unbearable to me,' he cried, little realizing what the consequences of such a request might be. In the middle of this time of inner turmoil Vanderkemp decided to move his family to Dordrecht where he hoped the climate would suit his health a little better.

A whirlwind

On one beautiful June day in 1791 John took Christina and
Johanna, now an attractive teenager, on a sailing trip up the
River Maas that flowed near his new home. Having enjoyed
a pleasant outing, the family at last turned homeward as
dark clouds began to gather. Then the sky rapidly blackened,
taking on a threatening aspect. Before they could make much
progress the heavens opened and torrential rain began to lash
down with a gale springing up. It tossed the little boat about
like a cork. Quite suddenly, with a roar, a whirlwind flung the
boat upside down and John, Christina and Johanna were all
thrown into the rough water. It was the last John Vanderkemp
saw of his girl. Unable to swim himself, he struggled valiantly
to keep hold of Christina. Twice he dragged her up from
below the surface and tried to cling to the upturned boat still
holding on to her; then he lost his grip of her once more.
Exhausted, he could only grasp hold of the keel and hope that
someone would come to his aid before he too succumbed to
the fury of the waves. At last, as the storm abated, John, the
sole survivor of the tragedy, was sighted by a passer-by and a
rescue was mounted.

Desolate, John Vanderkemp returned home alone—all he
had loved now gone. Surprisingly, on the Sunday following his
crushing sorrow he was to be found attending a communion
service. And far from rejecting him, here God met the
bereaved man. Face to face with the one whom he had
despised, John at last bowed his proud head and owned that
God had a right to take his wife and child. More than this, he
was brought to the place where he could give them up freely.
Then he went a step further still: 'I give myself with all that I

have entirely to you whose power and love I now feel.' At that instant he knew that 'the only religion that satisfies the soul consists of resting in Jesus.'

Bereft of all, John Vanderkemp now had all. He ate the bread and drank the wine with a believing heart. That was a never-to-be-forgotten communion service.

London Missionary Society

At forty-four John Vanderkemp knew that his best years of opportunity for service to God had already passed. During the closing years of the eighteenth century a heightened awareness of the needs of the unevangelized nations of the world had been steadily dawning on the Christian churches. William Carey sailed for India in 1792, the year after John's tragic losses. As he wondered what God wanted him to do, he heard thrilling accounts of the London Missionary Society, formed in 1795. He read of the courage of thirty young men and women who had left the security of home to sail to the far-off South Sea Islands. With a similar zeal Vanderkemp longed to serve God as they were doing but, tamed by his sorrows, he was less impetuous than before and wrote in his journal: 'I fell on my knees and cried, "Here I am, Lord Jesus. You know I have no will of my own since I gave myself up to you ... Prevent me only from doing anything in this great work in a casual and self-sufficient spirit."'

With expectancy and some apprehension, Vanderkemp wrote to the London directors of the new mission, enquiring about the possibility of joining with them in their endeavour. In an equally cautious reply, the directors invited the

Dutchman to come to London to discuss the opportunities. But, they told him, he must first consider the danger of wrong motives , coupled with the natural pride of the human heart. Did he have a sufficient awareness of the cost of such service for the kingdom of God, they asked? Rising to the challenge John decided to travel to England to meet the directors of the mission to have a face-to-face discussion. Impressed by his zeal and earnest spirit, his exceptional abilities, coupled with his equal facility in Dutch as well as English, the London Missionary Society accepted Vanderkemp for pioneer work in South Africa. The Dutchman would have the significant advantage of being able to communicate easily both with the officials of the Dutch East India Company (first settlers in the Cape) and the British who were then in possession of the Colony. The Society proposed, however, that before he embarked Vanderkemp should return home and raise concern in his own country for missionary enterprise and try to set up a Netherlands Mission on a similar basis to the London Society. This he did in 1797 and then, still eager to dedicate his remaining years to the spread of the gospel, he returned to London ready to sail with the next out-going missionary contingent due to leave English shores on the *Hillsborough* in December 1798.

Cape Town

The fifty-one-year-old Dutchman, now balding but still erect and alert, was to travel with three other missionary candidates as well as a sad and motley assortment of three hundred of Britain's unwanted citizens, felons and petty thieves alike, bound for exile in far-off Australia. Angry, dangerous and incarcerated in fearful conditions, these convicts presented a challenge to Vanderkemp's intrepid spirit. What did these men need more than the very gospel he was leaving home to proclaim? Despite mutinies, disease and death, the Dutch doctor could be found each day in the searing heat of the ship's hold befriending the convicts, gaining their respect, teaching them and providing basic medical help.

At last, after fourteen long weeks at sea, the *Hillsborough* anchored in the blue waters of Table Bay. For some months Vanderkemp and his fellow missionaries remained in Cape Town, acquainting themselves with the land of their adoption and its most pressing needs. Immediately the missionary doctor began to evangelize among the black slaves who formed almost half the population of the town. His fiery soul burned with indignation at the degradation suffered by these unfortunate people and the inhumanity with which the colonists treated them. The seed of future clashes between Vanderkemp and the local white residents was already being sown.

But Vanderkemp's present missionary purpose was twofold. First, he wished to press beyond the north-eastern borders of the colony to reach a particular warlike tribe called the Kaffirs, living in an area where few white men had yet ventured. And in the back of his mind lay another hope: one day he might also be able to bring the Christian gospel to the great island of Madagascar. His first aim, however, was to make contact with the tribal king to gain permission to live among his people.

Taking with him one of the other missionaries, a young

man named William Edwards, Vanderkemp set out on the long trek. Loading up their wagons with all they would need to plant a rudimentary mission station, the party set off. Across trackless desert, rugged hills and dried river beds they pressed, but all the time Edwards was growing more and more apprehensive. He would prefer to be a missionary in India he told Vanderkemp. At last they reached their destination and then began the laborious task of convincing the king of the local tribe to allow them to stay. Whether this tribal chief might smile on them or kill them appeared to depend on the daily fluctuations of his mood. At last the king agreed to assign land to the embryo mission, but at this point Edwards' nerve broke; he left his companion and returned to Cape Town. With large-hearted sympathy Vanderkemp understood the younger man's fears and provided money to help him with his fare to India.

Vanderkemp was now alone. The frail hut that he and Edwards had built for themselves was scarcely able to keep him dry, or save him at night from prowling hyenas and lions. But here he taught a people sunk in superstition and spiritual darkness to know the God he too had once despised. The duplicity and fickleness of the king, however, coupled with the harassment of roving white colonists made progress almost impossible. At last when the king decreed that the white doctor should be put to death, Vanderkemp decided he must seek opportunities elsewhere. A small group of Hottentots— the name given by the Dutch to the indigenous black population—had responded eagerly to the gospel message. These accompanied Vanderkemp on his slow progress back to Cape Town. There he discovered himself to be the focal point of accusations perpetrated by irritated white settlers who charged him with providing a refuge for their discontented farm labourers.

Bethelsdorp

With characteristic determination Vanderkemp was not unduly perturbed and now resolved to champion both the cause of the exploited Hottentot people and of the yet more downtrodden slave population. He would devote all his energies to their needs. Vanderkemp duly applied to the Dutch authorities, for the Cape Colony was now once more in their possession, for a grant of land to develop a mission station. Reluctantly a stretch of poor, infertile ground was conceded to the missionary doctor, but at least it presented a more settled and less dangerous situation than Vanderkemp had experienced in Kaffirland. There in the east of the colony he was gradually able to establish a strong and vibrant mission station which he named Bethelsdorp. Local black people attended the services he arranged and slowly but surely the number of conversions multiplied until another missionary was needed to help with the growing work. The mission station began to take on an established appearance as trees were planted, a church building erected and a school started.

Where a work of God is beginning to grow the devil is quick to use his malicious devices to halt it. Relationships between Bethelsdorp and the government now deteriorated further because of Vanderkemp's outspoken criticism of the cruelty with which the Dutch colonists treated the black population. Bethelsdorp was fast becoming an asylum for distressed and suffering people.

In 1804 Vanderkemp was summoned to Cape Town by the Dutch governor to answer incessant charges brought against him by white colonists that he was protecting black conscripts and slaves from their legal obligations to their Dutch owners. To add to Vanderkemp's problems he was strongly suspected of pro-English sympathies, as he had been sent to South Africa by an English missionary society. With war imminent between the Dutch and English for repossession of the Cape Colony, this added a serious dimension to the complaints of the white farmers. After a five-week trek Vanderkemp arrived in Cape Town only to discover that he and his fellow missionary were to be detained there indefinitely and prohibited from any further work at Bethelsdorp.

The days dragged on and still the missionaries waited. John Vanderkemp became deeply discouraged. In his depression he told a fellow missionary, 'I conceive that God has driven me from Bethelsdorp because of my transgressions and very likely I shall find no grace in his eyes to go back there again.' But God encouraged his servant with reassurances of his love and not long after he was able to testify: 'Last Friday I had a deep sensation of the satisfying power of Christ's righteousness and I found myself clothed by it from all sin ... I stepped boldly into the presence of God my Father who manifested himself in love to my soul.' Now he was confident that God would surely open the way for him to return to Bethelsdorp once again.

And so he did. On 4 January 1806 sails were sighted in the distance—British sails—and by evening more than sixty-three ships of war lay at anchor in strategic positions around Cape

Town. Unprepared, the Dutch governor tried hastily to gather his resources to mount a defence, but on 8 January the Battle of Blueberg was joined and by 18 January the Union Jack was once more hoisted over Cape Town. The new British governor considered Vanderkemp's cause sympathetically and soon he was on his way east, back to Bethelsdorp.

Entering the light

With an unusually cheerful spirit Vanderkemp returned to the work from which he had been summoned away. But there was a second reason for his buoyant mood. The fifty-seven-year-old missionary had fallen in love. With him he brought his young bride: a seventeen-year-old Madagascan girl. Pity, coupled with a strong empathy for the downtrodden and suffering slaves, had brought Vanderkemp into contact with Sara, a beautiful slave girl, while he was in Cape Town. His own life story was repeating itself. As with Christina, more than twenty years earlier, he found himself drawn out by Sara's youthfulness, helplessness and need. He used his own funds to buy her freedom and brought her back with him to Bethelsdorp. Not only did he pay to free Sara from slavery, he used the slender funds remaining in his own Dutch account to redeem her entire family from such inhumane bondage.

Vanderkemp had also a longer term project in view in his marriage to a girl from Madagascar. Ever since his arrival in South Africa he had hoped to reach the island with the gospel. His marriage would facilitate such an endeavour. Sara had responded to the truth he had taught her and was soon baptized as a believer. Four children were born in quick succession: three sons and a daughter. Cornelius, named after John's father, was the eldest, followed by Sidericus, then Africanus and lastly Sara Johanna—a reminder of the daughter he had lost.

Though Vanderkemp had longed to reach the people of Madagascar, God had other thoughts. At the age of sixty-four his work was done. The incessant opposition, his burning indignation at the treatment of slaves, the threats and dangers he had experienced had all taken their toll on his strength. He confessed to an increasing weakness and soon it was feared that the well-loved missionary doctor could not long remain in his work. It seemed that his young family must lose him. John Vanderkemp had been instrumental in bringing many black Africans into the kingdom of God and his brief work in South Africa had not been fruitless: his influence among the fierce tribal Kaffir people remained long after he had left. Side by side with the liberating gospel of Christ, Vanderkemp had believed passionately in the dignity of his fellow men and the right of the blacks for justice and equality.

As his weakness increased, it became apparent that Vanderkemp was indeed dying. 'What is the state of your mind?' asked a fellow missionary anxiously.

'All is well,' he whispered.

'Is it light or dark with you?' persisted his friend.

'Light,' came back the low answer.

And on 11 December 1811 John Vanderkemp entered that

light, leaving the shadows and injustices of earth behind for ever.

Marion Veitch

Proving God

In days when faithfulness to the truths of Scripture could and did cost men, women and young people their lives, Marion Veitch is a remarkable example of a woman who trusted God through dark days. Married to a Scottish Covenanter, she shared his sufferings to a marked degree.

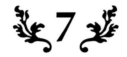

Marion Veitch

Proving God

Marion Fairlie, an attractive-looking Scottish girl was born in Edinburgh in 1639, a time when life was far from settled for the Scottish people. Twice during the following few years the nation was embroiled in conflict with the armies of Charles I of England as he, together with his henchman Archbishop Laud, tried to bring the Scottish church into line with Laud's High Church agenda. In view of all the conflict and uncertainty Marion's parents decided that Edinburgh was no longer a safe place to bring up a young family, moving to Lanark soon after the child's sixth birthday.

Marion was a thoughtful girl, and as she grew older she

became deeply concerned about her standing in God's eyes. To have parents who loved and served God might be good, but how could she know whether she herself had been accepted by him? When a visitor called at her home one day, Marion had just been praying that she might be given some inward certainty that she was a true believer. Entering the room where the adults were talking, Marion noticed that the visitor was holding a letter which he was about to read aloud. The girl had heard about the highly-acclaimed letters written by Samuel Rutherford, the Covenanter preacher from St Andrews, letters that were being secretly passed round from hand to hand. Instinctively Marion knew that this must be a copy of one of those letters which his correspondent was allowing others to read.

As the visitor cleared his throat and began Marion's interest was immediately quickened. The subject was the very thing that had been causing her such deep anxiety: how far is it possible to carry on appearing to serve God and yet be found to be a hypocrite at the last and merit eternal punishment? Marion did not know the answer. As she listened example after example was being given of Bible characters whose initial professions of faith had proved to be false: Esau, Balaam, Saul, Judas … Marion could bear no more. She slipped quietly out of the room—her mind in a confused whirl. For some days the inner battle raged. 'I will go to hell,' she thought in panic. 'But hasn't God promised that those who seek shall find him?' At last she came to a firm persuasion that God would show mercy to her for Christ's sake. And from that moment Marion never looked back throughout a long life packed with trials and uncertainties.

The troubles of the true church

As she grew to womanhood Marion's beauty attracted many would-be suitors. But to her only one thing mattered: she must marry a man who shared her faith. The troubles of the true church of Jesus Christ in Scotland had intensified, for in 1660, soon after Marion's twentieth birthday, Charles II had been invited back to the throne of England. Renewed persecution had immediately broken out against any unwilling to submit to the High Church agenda that was now being imposed on all the churches. August 24, 1662 was a grievous day. Known as Black Bartholomew's Day, it was the day that the Bill of Uniformity became law. More than two thousand English preachers were evicted from their livings because of their refusal to compromise their faith and to introduce innovations in worship that were demanded in the terms of the Act.

Two months later it was Scotland's turn. The Act of Glasgow was passed in Edinburgh by a semi-drunk Assembly, stipulating that every preacher who had not been ordained by a bishop must seek to be re-ordained at the hands of the bishops in conformity with the English *Book of Common Prayer*. More than four hundred Scottish preachers felt unable to comply with such a requirement and were also ruthlessly evicted from their livings. William Veitch, a young preacher who had been courting Marion, was among their number. To marry such a man would be to embrace a life of suffering, so Marion's friends warned her. But in her eyes his faith and courage spoke of deep devotion to the cause of Christ, and in November 1664, now twenty-four years of age, Marion married William. They settled at Dunsyre, sixteen miles south of Edinburgh.

In a sharply deteriorating situation, not only were the ministers suffering for their steadfast faith, but their congregations were too. Those who dared to slip secretly from their homes to hear their ejected preachers as they conducted services in many a hidden glen or on lonely mountainsides were subject to cruel reprisals. If they were caught or even suspected of attending such conventicles, as these outdoor services were they might be subjected to torture, inordinate fines and even shot on sight by the king's dragoons who roamed the countryside.

The peasant army

But in November 1666 a situation arose which would have yet more serious implications for William and Marion Veitch. At Dalry, in Galloway, an old man who had attended a conventicle had been seized by the dragoons. He was bound, whipped and was just about to be branded with red-hot irons when four men, hearing his cries, suddenly intervened on his behalf. The dragoons, taken by surprise, were quickly overpowered and bound themselves while the elderly man was released. Delighted at their unexpected success, the rescuers proceeded to march off with the captured dragoons. News spread quickly and others flocked from their villages to support the rout. Soon a makeshift army of peasantry had joined the revolt, William Veitch among them. But progress towards Edinburgh was gruelling and slow. Cold, hungry and exhausted, the peasant 'army' managed at last to reach the Pentland Hills near Edinburgh but there the uprising was ignominiously crushed by the superior forces of the king's crack troops.

Vengeance on all who had taken part in the rebellion was swift and cruel. When William did not return home, Marion, who now had the care of two infants and was expecting her third child, had little idea whether her husband was alive or dead. At last a message arrived telling her that he was on the run and would be heading for the safety of England. The search for William was relentless. Again and again the troopers hammered on Marion's door, often in the middle of the night. They would turn out cupboards, pierce through furnishings with razor-sharp swords and leave with a curse when once again Veitch could not be found.

Without her husband to care for her or to protect their young family, Marion was cast upon God in a new way. 'Trust in the Lord and fear not what man can do,' she wrote in her Memoirs, quoting from the Psalms, and this was her refuge and consolation through five difficult years. From time to time William took the serious risk of returning to his home for a brief, clandestine visit. On one such visit he advised Marion to move to Edinburgh where the family's presence would be more easily concealed. At last in 1671 a message came from Rothbury in Northumberland that William had managed to secure a living, preaching to a small congregation of non-conformists and it would be safe for Marion and the children to join him. With deep sadness she turned her back both on the Scottish scenes she had known from childhood and the sufferings of true believers still under the heavy hand of persecution.

Even in England Marion and William Veitch were not safe.
Vigilance was always needed for the King's troopers had
not given up the search. They could burst into the house at
any time on some tip-off, still looking for their man. When
circumstances forced the family to move to Long Horsley
the danger intensified, for the town was predominantly
Catholic and a Scottish accent quickly betrayed them. Narrow
escapes multiplied and on one occasion William only avoided
detection by armed justices of the peace as he hid behind the
curtains of a large window. But after three years of this cat-
and-mouse game William was captured. January 1669 was a
month Marion Veitch could not easily forget. At five o'clock
one morning as the family slept armed dragoons burst into
the house. William had no means of escape. 'You cannot go
one hair's breadth beyond God's permission,' Marion boldly
told the officer in charge as her husband was marched away at
gunpoint.

Kept at peace
The penalty for having been in that uprising in 1666 was
likely to be death. Marion knew this well enough. She had
no other recourse but to the God who hears the cries of his
people. With a family of six young children, one an infant of
only a few months old, she gave herself to constant prayer on
William's behalf. For twelve days William lay in the local jail.
Marion has recorded:

> At length God helped me to give him freely to him, to do
> with him as he pleased; and if his blood should fill up the cup
> of the enemy and bring about deliverance to his church, I

would betake myself to his care and providence for me and my children.

Comforted by words of Scripture and by a knowledge that all was under God's control, Marion was kept at peace. Then came a letter—one that she scarcely dared open—detailing the government's decision concerning William. He was to stand trial in Edinburgh, a virtual death sentence in itself. Leaving her children in the care of a friend, Marion hurried to the prison, but William was so closely guarded that she could not get near him. With bitter tears she faced the bleak prospect of her husband's conviction and likely execution. An inner battle raged, and as she quaintly expressed it, 'Faith brought me always good news, but when unbelief was master of the field it never had a good tale to tell of God.'

A month later the date for the trial was fixed. Marion travelled to Edinburgh to support William as best she could. Sometimes she was buoyed up with hopes that he might be treated leniently, but then she heard rumours that the death sentence was be the likely outcome, for William had been moved to a more heavily-guarded prison. Many events joined to make it unlikely that William Veitch would receive a light sentence, not least the determination of Charles II himself that this particular prisoner must perish. In addition, the murder of Archbishop Sharp, prime persecutor of the Covenanters, had taken place while the trial was in progress. This alone unleashed a demand for retribution on a prisoner like Veitch. But still Marion prayed and searched the Scriptures for consolation and strength. Throughout these days of intense distress, she clung to the God in whom she had trusted for so long. And God intervened on her behalf. Influential friends began to plead William's cause even to the king himself. They argued that if the death sentence were carried out, the repercussions in the land could aggravate the already fraught situation. At last the Privy Council gave its judgement: William Veitch would not be executed but would be banished from Scotland. Marion's relief was unbounded.

A tenuous freedom

Such a crisis of faith and prayer gave the persecuted Covenanter's wife an increased confidence in the God who answers prayer and a reference point to which her mind could return in every fresh trial and sorrow. Back in Northumberland William continued to farm his smallholding to support the family and preached wherever he had opportunity. But his freedom was tenuous. With every new spate of political unrest—and there were many in those troubled days the situation worsened. Despairing men and women were struggling to overthrow the unjust regime that was crushing their liberties and William Veitch came under constant suspicion of protecting desperate Covenanters from the cruel arm of the law.

These suspicions were not unfounded. When the Earl of Argyll made his astonishing escape from Edinburgh Castle in 1681, disguised as a pageboy, it was to the home of Marion and William Veitch's home that he came for refuge. Under the pseudonyms of Captain Forbes and Mr Hope, Veitch and Argyll set out for London, travelling together as far as the Midlands. Many were the narrow escapes they sustained together as the search for Argyll, the most wanted man in the country, became nationwide in its scope. On one occasion a notice was delivered to the very inn where the escapee was staying. It asked the innkeeper to question all his clients as the search for Argyll widened with a handsome reward offered for Argyll's capture. When Veitch and Argyll were questioned by the innkeeper they expressed delight at the thought of a reward and asked permission to search nearby inns for the prisoner. If they found Argyll, they assured the innkeeper, they would share the reward with him.

After Argyll's eventual escape to Holland, William returned home, but suspicions continued to follow him. Still weak from the birth of another child, Marion faced a further crisis as her husband was arrested and thrown into prison once more, accused this time of being implicated in a plot to overthrow the corrupt Stuart regime. Fragile and desolate, Marion searched the Scriptures for words of support. 'He is able to succour them that are tempted,' she read, and knew that her God would not forsake her in her need.

Leaving the country
When William was released, cleared of any involvement in the plot, he decided that the best solution would be to emigrate to the Carolinas together with his family until the situation in Scotland had eased. Marion was far from happy. How could she leave all that she had known and loved and forsake her own people, so many of whom were facing constant risks as they dared to listen to the 'field preachers'? As Veitch and others met to discuss their plans for emigration further trouble arose, for they were wrongfully suspected of gathering to hatch yet another plot against the king. With his life once

more in danger, flight was the only answer and this time Veitch decided to make for Holland. Two of William and Marion's sons were now teenagers and Marion thought that the boys would be safer if they joined their father. So with earnest prayers for their protection, she arranged for them to leave the country.

Alone once more with five young children, the eldest a twelve-year-old boy, and no regular means of support, Marion was cast on God for her every need. A threatening landlord and anxiety about her elder sons so far away gave her many 'errands' to the throne of grace. When John, her twelve-year-old, was taken seriously ill, her isolation and need was heightened. Instinctively she seemed to know that the lad was dying and her greatest concern was for his spiritual state. She earnestly prayed that even in his weakness John might cast himself on Christ for mercy. And God heard her cry.

'Mother,' called John. When Marion came to the boy's bedside he said, 'I have been praying and giving myself to Christ, and he answered me and took pleasure in my soul which has comforted me.' Then the child added, 'Isn't it a wonder that Christ Jesus should die for sinners?' Throughout John's remaining days he prayed often both for himself and for his brothers and sisters. When he was finding it difficult to speak, he simply held up one hand whenever Marion spoke to him of death and heaven. His last prayer was for his two older brothers that each might serve God in his life. 'Though we be far parted now,' he whispered, 'we shall meet in glory.' Calling his younger brother and sisters, he added a prayer for them and then said goodbye. Then with one hand lifted up, as he had done before, John was taken from all the sufferings of his short life.

As reports continued to flow from Scotland of the indiscriminate killing of men, women and even children without any certain proof that they had listened to or had protected the field preachers, Marion felt that she and her four remaining children would be safest in Newcastle rather than in Stanton, near Long Horsley, where they had been living for some time. She anxiously awaited news of William and the boys in Holland, but for many months none came. Again and again Marion turned to the pages of Scripture and took the promises and reassurances she found there as sure messages from God that all would be well, both with her move and with her family. 'There shall no evil befall thee, neither shall any plague come nigh thy dwelling,' she read and took courage once more.

In spite of all the personal anxieties which might legitimately have occupied Marion's prayers, her deepest concern was for the distressed state of the true church of Jesus Christ. The persecution had all but silenced the faithful preachers. Richard Cameron, one of the last and most fearless of the field preachers, had been ambushed and killed in 1680; Donald Cargill had faced martyrdom the following year, crying out as he faced death, 'Be not discouraged at the way of Christ and the cause for which I lay down my life.' Men like John Blackadder were still imprisoned on the Bass Rock; John Brown of Priesthill had been cruelly murdered before the eyes of his pregnant wife and children as he knelt in prayer, interceding for his enemies. The two 'Margarets', Margaret

Wilson and Margaret Maclachlan, one aged eighteen and the other seventy, had been tied to stakes and drowned by the incoming tide in the Solway Firth. Few apart from the young John Renwick were still ministering to the dispirited remnant who still dared to gather for worship, and there was a high price on Renwick's head.

Answers to her prayers

Day after day Marion gave herself to prayer that God would look in pity on his people in Scotland. Even though she had known many answers to her prayers she felt the need of new assurances of God's overruling providence in a dark situation. 'One night,' she later recalled, 'as I was pouring out my spirit before God on behalf of my native land, that he would not make them a desolation, I made use of this argument: that the great wickedness of those who were rulers in church and state might move him to cast them out. And I got these words for an answer, "Thy words are heard."' And so it was. In response to the cry of many, not only in Scotland, but throughout the country, God intervened on behalf of his people and in 1688 James II, brother of Charles II, was finally driven from his throne as William of Orange and Mary entered the country.

With the easing of persecution William Veitch was able to return from Holland with his two sons, now grown to be young men, and Marion was delighted in the reunion. She hoped to return to Scotland, but initially William ministered in a church in Beverley, Yorkshire, before returning first to Peebles in the Scottish Borders, and finally settling in Dumfries.

Despite all the privations, uncertainties and hardships that Marion and William Veitch had experienced in their lives, they both lived on into old age. They were never to be parted again, for they both died in 1722, with only a day between. They were buried on the same day. Marion Veitch's last recorded words sum up the spirit in which she lived:

I can say from experience, 'They that sow in tears shall reap in joy.' I have had more pleasure in praying for the accomplishment of the promises, than ever I had in possession. He has made me know his promise can neither die nor drown.'

John Cennick

Bold as a lion

Many who sing John Cennick's hymns know little about the man himself. Although ranking among the most outstanding preachers of the eighteenth-century revival, Cennick has not received the acknowledgement his labours and godly character deserve.

John Cennick

Bold as a lion

A small boy had been taken by his mother to visit her dying aunt. Entering the house before her, the child stopped abruptly, rooted to the spot. He had caught snatches of a conversation between two women, coming from his aunt's room.

'Mary,' said a tremulous voice which he recognized as his aunt's, 'I have something to say to you. You may think it is a lie, but indeed it is the truth. Last night the Lord stood by me and invited me to drink of the fountain of life freely.' John stood riveted as his aunt continued, 'And I shall stand before the Lord as bold as a lion.' Had he heard correctly? 'As bold as a lion?' How could anyone stand before God as bold as a lion?

He began to tremble. At that moment John's mother entered
the room. Anna Cennick approached her aunt's bedside,
saying tearfully, 'Poor soul!'

'Who dares call me poor?' asked the dying woman,
suddenly raising her voice. 'I am rich in Christ! I have got
Christ! I am rich.' Perhaps no one in that room thought of the
child, only about nine years of age, who stood there listening.
Nor could anyone have realized the impression that such a
scene might be making on him. 'The words she uttered indeed
pierced my soul,' John was to record many years afterwards.
'Bold as a lion,' he mused. 'Oh, that I might be assured of
heaven before I die!' Now he began to fear dying as he had
never done before, for he knew he had no such confidence
that God would ever accept him. Nor could he later recall
a single waking hour in the next seven or more years when
his aunt's dying words did not echo and re-echo through his
mind, creating unnamed longings.

An obstinate boy

Loyal members of the Church of England, George and Anna
Cennick had brought up their children strictly, insisting
on rigorous Sunday observance. But John Cennick, born
in Reading in 1718, was much like any other little boy the
world over. Sunday was not a happy day for him, for he
was required to spend many hours in reciting hymns and
prayers. This he then regarded as 'the worst bondage and
indeed cruelty', and looked enviously at his friends who
were free from such a burden. The daily routine of church
attendance did not improve the boy's behaviour. He lied
with the greatest ease until truth and falsehood became

almost undistinguishable in his mind. Looking back on his childhood, he described himself as an obstinate boy with a temper that could flare out of control at the slightest provocation. Petty theft from his school friends and acts of disobedience were regular happenings in his life. Yet despite it all, John had a sensitive conscience. If his behaviour had been particularly unacceptable during the day, he would dread going to bed at night lest he should find himself in hell when he woke. Urgently he would promise God that he would be good the next day. Religious though his parents were, they could neither guide their child to the Saviour nor tell him of one who could forgive sin and cleanse the guilty conscience.

By the time he was thirteen John Cennick's formal education was over. His family was not well off and it was essential that the boy should learn a trade. On eight separate occasions he travelled to London to try to obtain an apprenticeship; but each time was unsuccessful. So with little to occupy him, Cennick devoted himself increasingly to a way of life that was contrary to everything his parents had tried to inculcate. Good-looking and popular among his contemporaries, John had a flair for fashionable dress, and delighted to comply with the latest style. He buried himself in romances, thrilling tales of Roman and Greek culture, and developed a strong penchant for the theatre.

Only lack of money prevented him from spending all his time watching the best actors of the day. He would spend hours listening to the eighteenth-century equivalent of the latest pop music and wasting his pittance in gambling, always hoping to increase it by a wager. 'I had forgotten Jesus and everlasting ages, loving ungodliness more than goodness and to talk of lies more than righteousness,' was his later sad comment on these days. Yet despite everything, every day, every hour, he could not forget his aunt's dying words.

Heaviness of spirit

But if John Cennick was trying to push God out of his thinking, God had not forgotten him. It was Easter, 1735. Cennick was seventeen and still without any regular employment. As he walked hurriedly along the road in the Cheapside area of London, he was suddenly overtaken by a strange and inexplicable heaviness of spirit. He felt deeply depressed. Yet nothing had changed. His circumstances were exactly as they had been five minutes earlier. 'Have I neglected some religious duty? he wondered. Although such things meant little to him he had generally tried to maintain the outward semblance of such duties. Try as he might, he could not shake off the gloom that seemed to envelop him. Neither the theatre nor the songs he loved to sing brought him any relief. Perhaps the London air did not suit him. A spring day in the country would surely bring respite. But it did not. Perhaps God was singling him out for punishment because of his careless ways. John Cennick did not know. Again and again he thought of the happy confidence with which his aunt had died.

Days turned to weeks and weeks to months; still the blackness overclouded his naturally buoyant spirit. Returning home to Reading, he passed his time trying one distraction after another but the stubborn heaviness remained. At last he began to pray that God would come to his aid and wondered if he ought to turn his back on the world and enter a monastery. Nights were worse than the days: he woke out of sleep at every slight noise, fearing that this might herald the final Day of Judgement had come. Unwilling to face another day, he would sometimes lie in bed all morning or spend the time pacing backwards and forwards in his room. But of one thing he was sure: his problem was a spiritual one, yet he feared that God would reject the desperate prayers he offered up. Sometimes he would spend long days and nights wandering across Salisbury Plain, eating little apart from the wild berries that he found growing there.

No glimmer of light?
Two years passed in this way and still there seemed no glimmer of light to penetrate Cennick's mental gloom. He even envied the small animals he saw scurrying across his path on his lonely moorland walks and wished to die, yet feared the beyond. Now, however, his prayer had changed. It was no longer on the grounds of any fancied merit he might offer to God. Instead it was for the sake of the 'blood, tears and sufferings' of Jesus. The young man was nearing the end of his spiritual sorrows. Deciding it might be best for him to move from Reading and try to start life again elsewhere, Cennick prepared to leave his childhood scenes for ever. Then for the last time he heard the familiar toll of the church's old bell—that church he had attended daily from his earliest years. He decided to slip unnoticed into its cool shade and pray once more before he left. Kneeling there in deep despair, he paid little attention to the often-repeated refrain of the set prayers. Although lost in painful introspection, he suddenly caught the words of one of the Psalms that was being chanted:

'Great are the troubles of the righteous, but the Lord delivers him out of them all! And he that puts his trust in God shall not be desolate.' In that flash of a moment—a moment that cannot be calculated on any earthly time-scale, yet infinitely expansive on the time-scale of heaven—the thought crossed his mind, 'Who more desolate than I?' And then a surge of unutterable delight throbbed through his whole being:

> I was overwhelmed with joy and believed there was mercy. My heart danced for joy and my dying soul revived. I heard the voice of Jesus saying, 'I am thy salvation.' I no more groaned under the weight of sin. The fears of hell were taken away ... Christ loved me and died for me; I rejoiced in God my Saviour.

Later John Cennick expressed his experience in memorable words, words still to be found in many modern hymnbooks:

> This is the way I long have sought,
>   And mourned because I found it not;
> My grief and burden long have been,
>   Because I could not cease from sin.
>
> The more I strove against its power,
>   I sinned and stumbled but the more;
> Till late I heard my Saviour say,
>   'Come hither, soul, I am the Way!'

September 7, 1737 was a date never to be forgotten in nineteen-year-old John Cennick's life. For some hours he experienced a joy as intense as his misery had been profound. His first inclination was to share his relief and spiritual delight with those he thought would understand. But he had a surprise awaiting him. His family and friends were puzzled and even antagonistic to all he told them. Such religious zeal was unacceptable in those orthodox yet unenlightened circles.

Like most believers, Cennick did not experience uninterrupted peace of mind from that moment onwards. Subtle attacks of Satan, reminding him of his past, easily disturbed and troubled him and he was lonely. Misunderstood at home and regarded with suspicion by his acquaintances, he longed for someone with whom he could share his trials and joys. Even when a friend lent him a book to read, Cennick was deeply suspicious. His past reading habits had made him aware of the dangers lurking within the printed page for the unsuspecting reader. He glanced at the title and found that the book appeared to be the journals of someone called George Whitefield. Cautiously he began to read, but as he read he knew that at last he had found a kindred spirit—a soul mate. Here was one 'not unacquainted with the bitter cup, the dregs of which I had long been drinking'. Falling on his knees, John Cennick thanked God and begged that he might some day meet George Whitefield, and that when they met Whitefield would be prepared to speak with him and strengthen him in his lonely inner warfare. Before he had finished praying, however, a firm assurance gripped Cennick's mind that somehow, somewhere, they would meet.

'Kinchin by name'
A few months later he was at the house of one of his former companions who dealt out a pack of cards—a game that

had once given Cennick much pleasure and lost him plenty of money. Alarmed, Cennick refused to play, and instantly became the butt of the jokes of all in the room. 'There is just such a stupid, religious fellow in Oxford,' said someone, 'Kinchin by name ...' That was enough for John Cennick. He would walk immediately to Oxford and find this undergraduate called 'Kinchin'. Without knowing either which College he might attend, or even his first name, Cennick set out at his earliest opportunity on a forty-mile trek from Reading to Oxford.

Soaked to the skin, bedraggled and hungry, Cennick arrived at last within sight of the spires of the city. The folly of his excursion suddenly struck him. He had come all that way with only a surname to guide him to the man he was looking for. Was he crazy? He stopped to pray that God would somehow lead him to this Kinchin. After a miserable night in a poor boarding house, he spent the following day searching for his man. 'Is there a student here by the name of Kinchin?' he asked again and again. At last he met someone who knew John Kinchin.

'I hear you are despised on the same account as I am and should be glad to speak with you for a quarter of an hour,' Cennick ventured timidly when he and Kinchin met. That was a never-to-be-forgotten morning as he discovered his new friend was a member of a group known as the Oxford Methodists, or more derisively, as the Holy Club. From him he learnt about such men as John and Charles Wesley and George Whitefield. When he heard this name, Cennick's heart leapt for joy. Whitefield had been in America, so he was told, but was expected back in England shortly.

A bond of friendship

In November 1738, just a few weeks after his visit to Oxford, Cennick found out that George Whitefield had actually arrived and was staying in London with a printer named James Hutton. That very night he set out and walked from Reading to Hutton's home at Temple Bar. Much surprised to discover a footweary traveller standing on the doorstep at eight o'clock in the morning, Whitefield asked Cennick to come in and with typical kindness invited him to stay with him for several days. A bond of friendship sprang up between the two—a friendship that would have lifelong consequences for John Cennick. The younger man learnt of the amazing response of the miners in the Kingswood area of Bristol to the gospel preaching of Whitefield and John Wesley. Realizing the twenty-one-year-old's eagerness to serve Christ, Whitefield asked if he would be willing to become the master of a new school that was being built for the children of these miners.

Gladly Cennick agreed and in June 1739 walked the eighty miles to Bristol. The day after his arrival he made his way to Kingswood, where he understood a preacher was expected. Here he waited together with a significant number of miners. But no preacher arrived. At last someone suggested that the new young teacher might be able to give a 'word of exhortation' to the expectant people. Fearful, yet scarcely daring to refuse, Cennick begged the Lord to help him, and then addressed the miners. The response astonished him. Many were deeply affected and converted that very day. For

John Cennick there could now be no turning back. Despite being untrained and unordained, he had heard that inner compulsive voice of God calling him to be a preacher of the gospel. He knew he could well incur the disapproval of his new friends, but the die was cast that would mark out the course for the remainder of his life. His own words best express it:

Now shall I tell to sinners round
What a dear Saviour I have found!
I'll point to thy redeeming blood,
And say, 'Behold the way to God!'

Both Whitefield and Wesley expressed surprise when they learnt that John Cennick had started preaching. But it was a testimony to the stature of these men that they were able to see beyond the protocol of the church into which they had been schooled. Rather they were able to appreciate the greater good of the people of Kingswood who were eagerly responding to the messages they now heard from the young Cennick.

The enemy of souls

For eighteen months Wesley and Cennick worked together in harmony among the Kingswood miners; Whitefield was out of the country for most of the period. Sadly, as the kingdom of God was advancing apace, so the enemy of souls was active and the subsequent breakdown in relationships between Wesley and Cennick must be attributed primarily to the work of the evil one. Although doctrinal differences between Wesley and Whitefield sparked off the problem,

Cennick too was becoming increasing unhappy with some of Wesley's views. Misunderstandings multiplied and to avoid further divisions in the work, Wesley acted with radical speed. Coming to Bristol in February 1741, he called a meeting of the society and publicly dismissed his young assistant, forbidding him to preach again, either at the Kingswood School or among the believers gathered in the Kingswood Society. Meekly John Cennick complied. Remembering his fiery temper as a youth, we can see the change that had come to this young man through the grace of God. Only a dozen people accompanied Cennick as he looked for new premises where they could gather, but soon that dozen had grown to more than a hundred.

In March 1741 Cennick greeted George Whitefield's return from America with much pleasure. Whitefield would have learnt both with joy and sorrow of the experiences his young friend had faced in his absence. Generously he invited Cennick to help him out in the ministry in London at his new barn-like meeting house, known as Moorfields Tabernacle. Here Cennick met Howell Harris, the Welsh preacher, and a warm friendship sprang up between them. Similar in age, both had a burning zeal for the spread of the gospel; together they travelled to the villages of Wiltshire. For the first time John Cennick was to experience the mindless mob violence so familiar to the Welsh evangelist. Stones, dirt, filthy water, even blood from butchered animals would often be thrown at the courageous men. Disturbances of every sort were employed to drown the voices of the preachers.

On one occasion in June 1741, as they approached Swindon,

Cennick and Harris noticed a menacing-looking crowd beginning to gather. Nevertheless, they began the service with singing and prayer. Then gunshots began to ring through the air. Not in the least intimidated, the evangelists ripped opened their coats, and with bared chests declared to their gun-happy assailants, 'We are ready to lay down our lives for the gospel and would not resist if the guns were levelled at our hearts.' Such courage halted the crazy mob temporarily until a fire engine, a primitive device used to pump water from nearby ditches, was rolled up to try to silence them. But as they drenched Harris with ditch water, Cennick preached, and when the pumps were turned on Cennick, Harris preached. This continued for a further hour, soaking the preachers in turns until the pump itself broke down. At last the valiant pair could gain a hearing for their message.

Apostle of Wiltshire

But God was witness to all these indignities and sufferings endured for his sake. Sometimes those who had been foremost in persecution suddenly and unaccountably were stricken with disaster or death. Then the crowds began to fear, and persecution gradually died down. Known as the 'Apostle of Wiltshire', Cennick started to see fruit for his labours and afflictions. Where there had been cruel opposition, the people now crowded to hear him preach. Tytherton became his headquarters. For three years he evangelized throughout Wiltshire, seeing a remarkable work of God among the towns and villages until in 1743 a handsome chapel was erected in Tytherton. Called away temporarily from Wiltshire in 1744, Cennick was invited to oversee the pulpit at Moorfields Tabernacle for Whitefield who was about to return to

America. An onerous assignment, it was not one that Cennick found easy, and before long he was anxious to hand it over to Howell Harris who seemed more suited to the task.

Throughout these years the zeal and commitment of a group of Moravian Christians, whose early influence on both the Wesley brothers had been profound, were increasingly attracting Cennick. To him they seemed to represent all that was best in evangelical Christianity. He had met their leaders and had found a growing love in his heart for them. The emphasis which the Moravians placed on the person of Christ, and on his wounds and death for the sake of sinners, was one that stirred Cennick deeply. In 1746 he finally decided to cast his lot in with them.

After Cennick had visited the Moravian headquarters in Germany, he was accepted as one of their preachers and commissioned to work in Dublin. Leaving Wiltshire and also a girl there whom he was growing to love, Cennick crossed the Irish Sea. 'I shall never forget what I felt when I first stepped ashore,' he recorded in his diary. 'I could not refrain from tears, but prayed the Lord to stand by me in this strange country.' Neither Whitefield nor Wesley had yet set foot in Dublin's streets, but the way had been prepared for Cennick by praying men and women who welcomed him gladly to preach at their meeting place known as Skinner's Hall. Still only twenty-eight years of age, Cennick began to preach with a new measure of power as God did indeed stand by him. The people, largely nominal Catholics, thronged to hear him. Anyone who wished to have a seat had to be there at least three hours before a service was due to begin. The problem was that Cennick himself could not get into the hall. No solution could be found except for him to walk across the shoulders of the crowd and climb in through an open window.

Such an amazing work could not go unhindered, and soon missiles of all sorts were once again being flung at the plucky preacher. Turned out of their Skinner Hall meeting place by a deceitful act of a preacher who had once worked with Wesley, Cennick and his people quietly looked for alternative accommodation. Then came a call to leave Dublin and evangelize in the north of Ireland. Cennick's first experiences nearly cost him his life. Perhaps, thought the northerners, the young preacher was some traitor in disguise, an agent of the Pope's, maybe. In Ballymena an over-gallant soldier, with zeal inflamed with liquor, undertook to dispatch the 'rebel'. Blow after blow rained down on the preacher's head, and only the speedy reaction of his followers prevented the soldier's spear being thrust through his unarmed victim. Cennick realized it was not yet the time to preach in the north.

Across the Irish Sea

Returning to Dublin, he established his work in its new premises. Then he requested permission from the London Moravian Society who met in Fetter Lane to preach around more freely venturing beyond Dublin and sometimes returning to England and Wales. Not many months later he returned to Wiltshire once more where he claimed the patient Jane Bryant as his bride. But still the call to return to Ulster was high in Cennick's heart. At last in 1748 he felt it would be safe. Crossing the Irish Sea once more, together with Jane this time, he headed for Ballymena.

Orthodox but lifeless, these Ulster men were to prove more difficult to win for the gospel than the excitable Dublin crowds. Through secret hostility, misunderstandings and open opposition John Cennick battled on for the next five years. In barns, ruined churches or out in the open air with the rain and wind numbing both preacher and hearers alike, Cennick went on undaunted. Frequently he had insufficient food, and when he could not afford to keep his horse he would walk across wild terrain for many miles in search of needy men and women to reach with his message of mercy and the grace of God. With his attractive, boyish face and gentle ways, John Cennick won the hearts of his hearers, yet remained a powerful and fearless preacher. A number of his sermons have been preserved for us. In one he pleads:

You drunkards and rioters, you lovers of feasting and banqueting, come to the marriage feast of the Lamb. Jesus invites you to drink freely of the fountain of life and to eat the hidden manna. You who are fond of music, come and hearken to the Saviour for his voice is sweet.

Gradually the tide turned. Nowhere was the young preacher more loved than in Northern Ireland. Near Ballymena he was now addressing crowds of up to ten thousand eager hearers, and was besieged with invitations to return again and again. By 1752 ten chapels had been built and over forty societies established.

The high cost
But the cost was high. Physically John Cennick was worn out, though not more than thirty-four years of age. The injuries he

had received from drunken and enraged mobs, the meagre diet on which he often subsisted, the long hours of riding and preaching in wet clothes had all taken their toll. Even though he and Jane had the joy of two young daughters, Cennick had a growing conviction that his work on earth could be drawing to a close. In the early summer of 1755 Cennick opened a new chapel in Dublin—a permanent home for his growing congregations there. Then wishing to pay a further visit to Wales and to his friends back in Fetter Lane, London, he said a loving goodbye to Jane and the girls, and set off.

After some days his London friends were becoming anxious. John had told them he would write to let them know when they might expect him, but no news of him had been received. Then came a moment of relief. Cennick had just arrived, but their relief was short-lived. Hurrying out to greet him, his friends found him so ill he could scarcely dismount from his horse. 'I am extremely sick and feverish and I think my senses fail me a little,' he confessed. Overtaken by a high fever soon after leaving Ireland, he had ridden on for five days, scarcely eating, drinking or sleeping, hardly able to remain on his horse. One thing only mattered to him: he must reach Fetter Lane. 'Why didn't you stop when you felt the illness coming on?' his friends asked in bewilderment.

'I did not choose to lie down in a strange place. I wanted to reach home first,' was the simple reply.

For five days he lay, sometimes delirious, sometimes conscious, but never complaining. Not all that loving hands could do allayed the fever. When someone told him this illness could be his last, Cennick said quietly, 'I should like that best of all. I want to be taken to his arms.' From time to time they heard their beloved preacher murmuring, 'Dear Saviour, give me patience.' On 4 July 1755 John Cennick heard the call to come, drink of the fountain of life freely and like his aunt so long ago, he also left the scene of all his earthly toils, sorrows and joys to stand bold as a lion before the throne of God. He was thirty-six years of age.

Ruth Clark

In service to Jesus Christ

When a young servant girl can draw highest praise from one of the most honoured and well-known preachers of the past, it is worthwhile finding out more about her. Ruth Clark, transformed by the grace of God, served all her life in the household of Henry Venn and his family.

9

Ruth Clark

In service to Jesus Christ

Fiery, competent and industrious, Ruth Clark worked as a domestic servant for Henry Venn, a man who ranked among the most outstanding preachers during the eighteenth-century evangelical revival. 'Ruth is my servant,' remarked Henry Venn to his children on one occasion, 'but if your father is found at her feet in the great day, his rank will not be a low one.' A girl who could draw so warm an accolade from a man of Venn's discernment and godliness deserves a permanent place in the record books of noble Christian men and women of earlier generations.

By birth Ruth came from a comfortable, even well-to-do, home in Leeds, Yorkshire, and the thought that any of their ten children would be forced to earn a living in domestic service would have been quite alien, even appalling, to Ruth's parents. Well-educated and wealthy, Ruth's father had prospered in business, and in childhood Ruth, who was born in 1741, played with Joseph and Isaac Milner, brothers who were to rank among the most erudite and spiritually influential men of the entire century. But Ruth's father was a restless speculator in a generation of gamblers and speculators. In his youth the nation had been shocked by the dramatic failure of the South Sea Company, when men saw their fortunes vanish overnight with the bursting of the 'South Sea Bubble'. It seems that Ruth's father had not heeded the warning and shortly before the birth of his tenth child, due to his own folly, he saw his family fortunes plummeting. Unable to face the humiliation of his losses, he walked out of his home, never to return; never to be heard of again. Ruth's mother was left alone to face the birth of her child and the care of her numerous family.

Early responsibility

Ruth was the second child in the family and was little more than ten when her father disappeared. While her elder sister immediately set out to seek employment in one of the houses of the local gentry, Ruth found that she could earn a small income by undertaking spinning tasks in the home, and so was also on hand to help her mother. Broken with anxiety not only by the financial distress, but even more by the loss of her husband, Ruth's mother could not regain strength following the birth of her child and remained virtually bedridden for many months. The burden of the family fell increasingly on Ruth's young shoulders. When her mother died several years later, Ruth, now a young teenager, had to bear much of the responsibility for her brothers and sisters.

The girl found that she needed to obtain employment in order to earn enough to contribute towards the support of the family. Bright, competitive and strong-minded, she soon gained a reputation as a hard and efficient worker. The home where she found employment had a back courtyard that opened out on to the street. From here Ruth could see into the backyards of the homes of other families who also employed domestic help. The girls working in all these different homes would compete with one another to see who could be the quickest to finish the Monday wash; their triumph indicated by being first to display an emptied and drying washtub. So seriously did Ruth take this challenge that she would not undress on a Sunday night and scarcely slept, springing up well before dawn to start the wash. Her employer, who had herself once been a cook in a well-to-do household, initiated Ruth into the secrets of cookery and home management until she excelled at these skills as well.

To work for a Methodist
Not long after her eighteenth birthday Ruth Clark was in need of another job. Her reputation in the kitchen was now well established and so, when Henry Venn was appointed as the new vicar of Huddersfield in 1759 and moved there together with his wife and young family, Ruth was recommended to him.

'You are going to work for a Methodist,' taunted her friends. 'They do nothing but preach and pray.'

'What's a Methodist?' thought Ruth in alarm. So apprehensive was she that she called on the one who had recommended her to Venn and asked nervously what she might expect.

'Go and judge for yourself, Ruth, and never mind what people say,' was the answer she received. 'I predict you will never leave the service of such a master if you once try him.'

And so it proved. But it was not all plain sailing. Each morning her new master called all the household together for an act of worship before the day began. 'What a waste of time!' thought the young mistress of the kitchen. She began to think of all the tasks she could have performed during the time Venn was addressing them or praying. The only way she could overcome her boredom was to count the flowers on the wallpaper to divert her mind.

Ruth had a temper that could flare out of control at the slightest provocation, and Henry Venn was repeatedly obliged to correct his irascible servant girl. But the efficiency, speed and excellence with which she worked put her skills and service beyond reproach. Most of all, Venn was troubled about Ruth's spiritual state. She seemed so proud, so eager to impress others and, at the same time, quite heedless of the truths he was preaching from his Huddersfield pulpit and in his home. But he was wrong if he thought Ruth was unaffected. One event more than any other touched the girl deeply.

Ernestly seeking the Lord

In 1767, when Ruth was twenty-six, Henry Venn's wife was taken suddenly and seriously ill. With a burning fever it was soon evident that this godly woman would shortly be taken from her husband and her five young children. Ruth could not fail to be reminded of her own mother's circumstances, but here she witnessed suffering eased by the strong consolations of the Christian faith both on the part of Henry Venn and of his dying wife. Even in her final days she was concerned for others and particularly for Ruth. Calling her to the bedside, Mrs Venn addressed her affectionately and earnestly: 'In what state should I have been if I had not a Saviour to look to? Make it your first concern, Ruth, to be prepared for death and trifle no longer with your soul.'

Above all, Ruth was affected by the way Henry Venn himself reacted to his loss. Writing to his friend, Selina Countess of Huntingdon, who had invited him to spend some days at her home in Bath following his bereavement, Venn could say:

> Did I not know the Lord to be mine ... into what a deplorable condition should I have been now cast ... I have lost her when her industry and ingenuity and tender love and care of her children were all just beginning to be perceived by the two eldest girls ... Nevertheless I can say, 'All is well! Hallelujah! For the Lord God omnipotent reigns.'

He refused the invitation because he did not want to leave the children or Ruth at that time, and could describe the latter as one who was now 'earnestly seeking the Lord'. He feared that if he went away the loss of the regular time of family worship which had become 'sweet indeed' to Ruth would put back the progress of the gospel in her life.

As she was always up before dawn (without the advantages of electricity people would retire much earlier in the evening), Ruth would often hear her master singing hymns quietly to himself at four in the morning even though it was only a short time after his wife had died. Her first task of the day was to clean Henry Venn's study, and sometimes she had not finished when he would arrive at five o'clock. Ruth was deeply impressed with the look on his face. Clearly he had been praying. Later she was to say that he reminded her of Stephen when confronted by his malicious critics, whose face was said to be like the face of an angel (Acts 6:15).

On several occasions Venn challenged Ruth about her spiritual state, but the subject distressed her for she imagined that his gentle probing indicated that he had given her up as hopeless. Yet in secret she was praying earnestly that Christ would not also give her up. Wisely Venn watched and waited and did not press Ruth unduly. Each time her fiery temper disturbed the peace of the household, the young woman was plunged into deeper despair. Eventually there came a day when Ruth was listening to a sermon in Venn's Huddersfield church, preached by a friend of his. She saw at last that Christ had come to save sinners: the gift of salvation was not reserved for those who had achieved some prescribed degree of righteousness. Tears ran down her cheeks as she realized both the depth of her sinfulness and the strength of the pride and self-righteousness that had hindered her for so long. But these were also tears of joy as she knew her past had been forgiven for Christ's sake.

An even better servant

Not easily nor all at once did Ruth Clark overcome the sin of an uncontrolled temper and a caustic tongue. When Henry Venn overheard Ruth and another member of his domestic staff quarrelling loudly, he was saddened. Calling Ruth aside he told her plainly that 'such sins made him suspect the sincerity of her religion'. His comment pierced Ruth's heart like a dagger, and she wept bitterly as she knelt alone in her room. She had failed again. And her master's doubts 'filled her with gloomy apprehensions'. But God himself comforted the forlorn young woman as she recalled a verse of Scripture: 'Though Abraham be ignorant of us, and Israel acknowledge us not: thou, O Lord, art our Father.' God knew her heart, and recognized the sincerity of her longing to please him, despite her failures.

With her natural determination and new spiritual desires, Ruth gradually mastered her boisterous personality. Those who knew her in later years could scarcely imagine that she had once given way to repeated bursts of anger. A good servant before, she was now an even better one. She became trustworthy even in the smallest details of daily management of the kitchen. Wishing to 'borrow' a small cup of milk on one occasion to give to someone in need, she ensured she had gained permission first. Her fierce independence remained and she would always refuse help with her tasks, insisting she could manage however great her workload. When Venn's curate John Riland married, he and his bride came to live at the vicarage, increasing Ruth's duties. In addition, the vicarage was sometimes crowded with visitors: men like John Wesley, George Whitefield, John Fletcher or even the Countess of Huntingdon and her entourage, would come to share days of fellowship with her master. Once with eighteen extra sheets to wash in her well-scrubbed washtub, Ruth locked herself in the laundry room until the chore was finished.

Move to Yelling

In 1771 there came a great change in Ruth's life and also in the lives of all the family in Huddersfield. Henry Venn, who had suffered prolonged ill-health, had accepted a call to a church in the village of Yelling, not far from Cambridge. Ruth unhesitatingly decided to accompany the family to their new home even though it meant leaving all she had ever known in the north of England. After the crowded congregations in Huddersfield, Venn now found he had only twenty or thirty villagers to whom to preach, most with little if any knowledge of the gospel. Over the years of his ministry in Yelling, the situation would change markedly, and one significant factor in that change was the unobtrusive and largely unrecognized influence of Ruth Clark.

Far from the bustling duties of a town vicarage, the country rectory presented Ruth with different challenges. She took on a ministry all of her own in her special concern for many deprived and sick villagers. Having experienced in her personal life the fears and uncertainties of extreme poverty, her sympathy and concern gave her a ready entrance to homes where the door might not be opened to the Rector. Ruth's loving interest was still remembered in the village twenty-five years after the close of Venn's ministry. 'Didn't you have a most wonderful servant?' asked Venn's successor in Yelling when he met a member of Venn's family. 'She seemed to be the mother of the whole parish by their account of her.'

Ruth delighted to keep her kitchen spotless. Her brass pans were buffed up until they shone like mirrors. The floors were scrubbed with regular diligence. So when Henry Venn suggested that he would like to invite the villagers into Ruth's kitchen each evening for a service of worship, it would not be hard to imagine that the thought of fifty or more pairs of mud-laden boots trampling across her gleaming floor, depositing their evidences of a day's toil in the fields on the chairs and stools, might present a problem for Ruth. When her new mistress, Venn's second wife, spoke kindly to Ruth regretting all the extra work it caused her, her cheerful reply demonstrates the remarkable change that her conversion had brought: 'Never mind, Ma'am; what does it signify if the people do but get good to their souls?' All the same, the moment the last villager had left, Ruth's sharp little knife came out as she began scraping all the mud off her chairs and washing her floor yet again. Her warm support for Venn's kitchen meetings was undoubtedly a great encouragement to him.

As word of the new ministry in Yelling began to spread, so the congregations grew. Students from Cambridge would walk the twelve miles to hear Venn preach and ask his advice, while men and women from the surrounding villages added to the numbers in the pews. Some came from distances that made it difficult for them to return to their homes for a meal; it was Ruth who welcomed them into her kitchen and provided a Sunday dinner for many hungry people, in addition to cooking for the family. And her provision for the parish was not restricted to Sundays. Always economical, she would boil up bones together with any leftovers and have an ever-ready stockpot to provide soup for the sick or needy.

Willing service

The secret of Ruth Clark's willing service for others lay in her personal communion with Jesus Christ. Having seen in the face of her master, Henry Venn, the serenity that comes from a close fellowship with God, this became part of her own constant practice. Not in a position nor of the temperament to spend long hours in devotion, she nevertheless maintained regular times of prayer. Her apron had a large pocket and in it Ruth always kept her Bible and hymnbook. As she worked she would sing to herself and doubtless such words as these written by Charles Wesley could often be heard coming from the kitchen:

Jesus, confirm my heart's desire,
To work and speak and think for thee;
Still let me guard the holy fire,
And still stir up thy gift in me.

Now living far away from her own family, who had mostly remained in the Leeds area, Ruth did not forget them, or their material and spiritual needs. She wrote many letters full of news of spiritual advice both to her brothers and sisters and to their children. Often she would include a small book that might be helpful. The 'spiritual advice' for the children was almost always accompanied by some small gift, for as Ruth explained, this would make them 'more inclined to receive in good part whatever else I send'. Her generosity did not stop there. When one of her brothers died, his four orphaned children were likely to be taken to the workhouse. This was the most dreaded of all fates and without hesitation Ruth sent her entire savings to the family to prevent that from happening. When a kindly neighbour agreed to care for the children, she arranged for a regular sum to be taken from her wages for their provision. This costly kindness meant that Ruth herself was left with virtually nothing for her own support in old age.

While Ruth was still in her fifties she succumbed to a condition for which there was no known cure at the time. Its exact nature is uncertain, it might have been diabetes or even epilepsy, but it left Ruth far less able to perform the service she had so freely given to others before. Unable to know when she would be taken ill, she hesitated to attend the services at the church in case her condition should disturb the worship. Always fiercely independent, Ruth's ailment now made her dependent on others—a situation she found hard to bear. Now she had to learn the lessons of submission in times of suffering, and to seek deliverance from the temptation to complain about her lot.

To add to her anxiety, her master, Henry Venn, whom she had grown to love deeply was fast failing. It was clear that his ministry was coming to an end. At last the family insisted that he should relinquish his Yelling pulpit and live in Clapham with his son, John, who at this time was also in the ministry.

In kindness John Venn asked Ruth to accompany his father and she soon found many tasks she could do in the Clapham household. Henry Venn had only six months to live and his death in 1797 was a bereavement that touched Ruth deeply. 'Oh, ma'am,' she said to one of Venn's daughters, 'when one gets to heaven, to see the Saviour, that will be first! It would not be heaven without him; but then next to see my dear and honoured master, what a joy and delight!'

No fears or doubts

Ten more years of life were left to Ruth after her master's death and the Venn family provided for her to the end. The money she had given away to her brother's children would never be missed. She spent her last years in Brighton cared for by Eling Elliott, the eldest of Henry Venn's daughters. Loved by Eling's children, one of whom, Charlotte Elliott, would become a well-loved hymn-writer, Ruth would spend time with them, and often retell the familiar Bible stories. And she was not beyond giving Eling herself a little homely advice on economy in the kitchen and the best way to provide for her household.

As Ruth crossed a road in Brighton one day in 1807, she was startled by the loud rattle of a horse and cart coming towards her at great speed. With no time to escape from the danger, Ruth was knocked to the ground. The accident precipitated a much more serious illness, and at the age of sixty-seven Ruth's desire to see her Saviour was soon to be fulfilled. 'It is hard work to die,' she confessed to one of the Venn sisters who was visiting her, 'but I have a hope which is able to support me.'

'Have you any doubts?' asked her visitor.

'Oh no, none,' Ruth replied. 'He that has loved me all my life through will not forsake me now. I have no rapturous feelings, but I have no fears or doubts.'

And so Ruth Clark, Henry Venn's faithful servant, but yet more, a servant of the Lord Jesus Christ, went to her true Master in May 1807. She was buried in the same grave as Henry Venn himself—a mark of the honour in which the family held her.

William Tennent

Caught up into paradise

William Tennent's father could be described as the founder of Princeton Theological Seminary, even though lectures were only conducted in a log hut at the time. His sons, all taught by their father, had distinguished ministries in New England and William's life, in particular, was of outstanding worth and interest.

William Tennent

Caught up into paradise

Grieving friends and relatives gathered to attend the funeral service. William Tennent, a young man of unusual promise and ability was dead. Only twenty-two, William was a theological student in New Jersey who had been studying under the oversight of his older brother, Gilbert. But it had become clear that the intense study was gradually undermining William's health. Pains in his chest coupled with serious weight loss had troubled friends and family alike. To make matters worse William had been growing increasingly uncertain about his own spiritual standing before God, fearing that if his illness led to his early death he would find himself rejected by God at the last.

Then one day while William and Gilbert were on their own together, they began discussing the younger man's fears. Quite suddenly William collapsed on the ground. Lifting his limp body in his arms, Gilbert carried him gently into another room and laid him down. William was pronounced dead. Was it a heart attack? No one was sure. William's doctor, also a close personal friend, happened to be away from home at the time, but when he returned and heard the news he was deeply distressed. Hurrying to where the body was lying awaiting burial, he insisted on conducting a further careful examination—and was far from satisfied with the results. He thought he could detect an unusual warmth under one of his patient's arms and demanded that the funeral should be delayed. Meanwhile the body was moved to a warm bed.

For three days and nights, the doctor remained by William's body doing all in his power to discover whether in fact there was any life. On the third day the funeral party reassembled. But still the doctor pleaded for time. Despite the cold, stiffened limbs and sunken eyes he clung to the faint, though now receding, hope that his friend was not dead. Gilbert could stand the strain no longer and, snapping at the young doctor, accused him of absurdity. Just one more hour then, begged William's doctor friend: half an hour; quarter of an hour; five minutes. As that last moment ticked by there came a sound, a groan from the bed. Then the 'dead' man's eyes flickered open for an instant, and closed again. All thoughts of burying William Tennent were now abandoned as every effort was bent towards reviving him from his comatose state. A slow recovery followed, but it was more than a year before William regained his strength.

Emigration

William Tennent had been born in Armagh, in Ireland, in 1705. When his father, also called William, felt he could no longer worship in accordance with the dictates of the Established Church, he and his wife, together with eleven-year-old William, his three brothers and sister, emigrated to America in search of religious liberty. The family settled first in New York and then moved to Pennsylvania when William Tennent, senior, was called to become the pastor of a small congregation at Bensalem. In 1726 the family moved once more, this time to nearby Neshaminy. William Tennent, senior, was a man of exceptional ability who taught his four sons at home, each of them becoming proficient in the classical languages and theology. When his sons' education was almost complete, he began to instruct other young men living nearby who wished for a theological training. With growing numbers he built a log cabin next to his home as a primitive theological college. This picturesque building became known as the Log College, and would become the forerunner of the great Princeton Theological Seminary.

Not all loss

When Gilbert, the eldest of the Tennent sons, entered the Christian ministry in New Brunswick, his brother, William, two years younger than Gilbert, also moved in order to study for the ministry under Gilbert's supervision. Then came William's strange illness and apparent death. As he regained strength he discovered that everything he had previously learnt had been wiped from his mind like chalk from a washed slate. He must start all over again. First, he had to learn to walk, then to speak and finally to read. On one occasion he noticed his sister looking at a book.

'What book is that?' he asked.

'It is a Bible,' she replied.

'What is a Bible?' asked William.

His sister wept, realizing that her brother's extensive knowledge of the Scriptures, of Hebrew, Latin and Greek, of theology, together with all his memories had been forgotten. But William Tennent's near-death experience was not all loss—far from it. For many years he was most reticent to speak about what had happened to him during those days that he had lain apparently dead. Long after, he gave a friend a vivid account. He told him that while Gilbert and he had been discussing his own spiritual fears, he had suddenly found himself 'in another state of existence' as he expressed it. He was being guided along by a 'superior being' whom he was commanded to follow.

I was accordingly wafted along, I knew not how, till I beheld at a distance an ineffable glory, the impression of which on my mind it is impossible to communicate to mortal man. I immediately reflected on my happy change, and thought, 'Well, blessed be God! I'm safe at last, notwithstanding all my fears.' I saw an innumerable host of happy beings surrounding the inexpressible glory, in acts of adoration and joyous worship; but I did not see any bodily shape or representation in the glorious appearance. I heard things unutterable. I heard their songs and hallelujahs of thanksgiving and praise with unspeakable rapture. I felt joy unutterable and full of glory.

He then asked for permission to join that joyful multitude. 'No,' replied his guide gently, 'you have to go back to the earth.' The words pierced through William's heart like a sword. And the next moment he became aware that his brother, Gilbert, and his doctor friend were arguing about something. So great was the shock of having to return to a world of tears and sin that he fainted several times before regaining full consciousness. Those three days seemed to him to have been only ten or twenty minutes in duration. Never could he forget what he had seen and heard:

> The ravishing sound of the songs and hallelujahs that I heard, and the very words uttered were not out of my ears when awake, for at least three years. All the kingdoms of the earth were in my sight as nothing and vanity; and so great were my ideas of heavenly glory that nothing which did not in some measure relate to it could command my serious attention.

Life Work

Gilbert spent many hours teaching William the biblical languages, theology, Latin and other branches of learning all over again. But one day, as he was reciting a Latin exercise, William suddenly clasped his hand to his head as if he had felt a stab of pain. 'What's the matter?' he was asked. The answer was extraordinary. He replied that the book from which he was reciting looked strangely familiar to him. He was sure he had read it before. He had. Gradually all his previous knowledge returned, together with clear recollections of his earlier life.

Not until 1733, however, five years after his illness, did William Tennent feel he was ready to be ordained and to enter the life work for which he had been preparing. When the death of his younger brother, John, left a congregation in Freehold, New Jersey, without a pastor, the church approached William, asking him to fill the vacancy. For forty-four years he faithfully served that one congregation.

Although Tennent's stipend at Freehold was modest, coupled with it was farmland belonging to the church. With careful cultivation this could adequately supply his needs, but William had little interest in temporal affairs. At times he seemed heedless, even careless, of anything apart from the concerns of the spiritual realm. He left the management of his business to a steward who not only farmed his lands but also dealt with his finances. This arrangement gradually proved unsatisfactory, and before long the steward was reporting that serious debts were mounting up.

Hardly knowing what to do, Tennent mentioned his predicament to a friend who was visiting him. This friend had a very practical answer to the problem. 'You must get married,' he replied The love and assistance of a level-headed woman seemed the obvious answer to Tennent's problems.

'But,' protested the embarrassed man, 'I have no idea how to go about a courtship, nor have I time for such things in any case.'

His friend had a ready answer. His own sister-in-law, recently widowed and about the same age as Tennent, was both practical and sincere in her Christian devotion. She would make him an excellent wife. If William would accompany him to New York the following day, he would introduce him to the lady in question and prepare the way for him. And so he did. William liked the look of Mrs Noble, but told her he was too busy for a courtship. He would return the following week, and if she agreed to his proposal, they would marry immediately and she would then return home with him. Not surprisingly, Mrs Noble was staggered at such a strange suitor. Nor was she at all sure that she even wanted to marry William Tennent. With just a week to think about it, she decided, however, that in view of all the circumstances it was the right thing for her to do. As good as his word, William returned the following week, and when Mrs Noble agreed to his request, they were married and went back to Freehold together.

The new Mrs Tennent immediately set about organizing William's affairs. She extricated him from debt, fed him satisfactorily, and proved an admirable wife in every respect. Soon a son was born to them. As William was taking his three-year-old for a walk one day, he began to think of the child's future. What would happen to this small child and to his wife if he were to die? What provision had he made for them? Then God showed him that despite his profound sense of the value of eternal things, he had been wrong to neglect the temporal affairs of life as he had done. Deeply convicted of his unbalanced attitudes, William began to view these God-given duties from a different perspective.

Manifestation of the Gospel

These were remarkable days in the American Colonies—
days of spiritual awakening when men such as Jonathan
Edwards, Samuel Davies, Samuel Blair and many others
were experiencing unusual blessing on their preaching.
The youthful George Whitefield was travelling the country,
attracting immense crowds wherever he went. A strong
awareness of spiritual realities was abroad. Not long after the
outset of Tennent's ministry at Freehold, God privileged the
young pastor with a further sight of his glory—and like his
former experience, one that would leave an indelible stamp
upon him.

Both the Sunday services at Tennent's church were normally
held close together with only half an hour's break between.
On this particular occasion Tennent was walking in the
nearby woods during the interval. As he walked he was
meditating on the astonishing wisdom of God both in
creation, but even more in the sufferings of Christ for sinners.
The more he thought about these things the more amazed he
became. Then a sudden and unexpected flood of divine glory
seemed to pour over him. Staggered, he fell to the ground,
overpowered by a realization of God's infinite majesty and
his own total unworthiness. His physical frame was scarcely
able to sustain the burden. All he could do was to beg God to
withdraw his shining presence, for the pressure on his soul
was so intense he feared it would kill him.

There he lay, too overcome to move; and there his elders
found him when they came in search of him. Gradually
they helped Tennent to his feet and half-carried him to his

pulpit into which he climbed on his hands and knees. The congregation watched in silent astonishment, baffled to know what had happened. As his strength began to return, Tennent grasped hold of the pulpit desk to help him to stand and then in terms simple but deeply affecting, he told the people as best he could of this amazing outpouring of the Spirit of God on his soul. None present could easily forget that day.

Such a manifestation of God had a lasting impact on Tennent's ministry. Remarkable anecdotes have survived of the power that accompanied his preaching. Many of his hearers wept as they realized their sinfulness in the sight of God. He did not time his sermons by his watch. Sometimes he could hardly stop; but at another time a friend who had walked twenty miles to hear him preach remarked that the sermon lasted no more than thirteen minutes! During these years the congregation at Freehold increased rapidly, not only numerically but in godliness and devotion to Christ.

Like all whose ministry threatens the kingdom of darkness, Tennent experienced times of severe temptation. As he was preparing a sermon one Saturday evening, a thought pierced his mind like a poisoned arrow: the Bible is not divinely inspired; it is just a figment of human imagination. He struggled to resist the temptation through prayer, but it seemed as if God had turned away from him. The conflict intensified. Even when he entered his pulpit the following day the battle was as fierce as ever. As the service continued the blackness surrounding his spirit grew even more oppressive. He scarcely knew how to go on. Then came the moment when he had to lead in prayer. Lifting his arms heavenward Tennent cried out in despair, 'Lord, have mercy on me.' Light from heaven flooded his soul, and as he proclaimed the absolute certainty of God's Word, tears poured down many cheeks. On that one day some thirty people professed conversion.

A trial

If the evil one could not prevent Tennent's usefulness by his fiery darts, he had other weapons in his arsenal with which to silence him. A local rogue, Tom Bell, ingenious and wily, bore a striking resemblance to a certain John Rowland, one of the New Jersey preachers. Dressed in clerical garb, Bell enjoyed impersonating the preacher whom he resembled. On one occasion he accepted an invitation to preach in a town where Rowland was not very well known. As Bell rode to the church on his host's handsome mare he suddenly said that he had forgotten his sermon notes and must go back to the house to fetch them. Returning to an empty house, Bell ransacked the place for valuables and rode off on the mare. But John Rowland, not Tom Bell, was arrested and charged with burglary.

In reality John Rowland had been staying with William Tennent and two other friends in Maryland at the time on some church business. When the case came to court, Tennent and his two friends appeared for Rowland as witnesses to the fact that on the day of the robbery Rowland was with them and far from the scene. On this testimony Rowland was acquitted, but the man who had been robbed and many others were quite convinced that Rowland was indeed guilty. Therefore, the spotlight was turned on the three who had spoken for him: they must be guilty of perjury. Tennent and his companions were arraigned to appear before the quarter sessions where by a total travesty of justice, they were declared guilty. The case must now go before a jury at the Supreme Court to be held at Trenton. The first of the three to be tried was again judged to be guilty, and ordered to stand for an hour on the court house steps holding up a notice which read: 'This is for wilful and corrupt perjury.'

William's brother, Gilbert, and two of the best lawyers in the area came to court to try to speak in William's defence. The third defendant had taken advantage of a less-than-honest exemption clause and had been acquitted. Only Tennent remained to face the charge of perjury. It was vital, his lawyer told him, that he should produce witnesses to prove that he was actually where he said he had been at the time. Without witnesses he could not hope to be acquitted. But Tennent knew of no one who could give any such testimony for him. As he walked to the court he heard the bell toll that indicated that proceedings were about to begin. In his mind he faced the full horror of a guilty verdict being passed on him with all the harm it would do to his Christian profession and ministry.

Just at that moment a man and his wife came hurrying up. 'Is your name Tennent?' asked the man.

'Why, yes,' replied the preacher. 'Have I any business with you?'

The couple came from Maryland, from the very town where William had spent the days in question. They were servants in the house where Tennent and his friends had stayed. A few nights earlier, so they told him, both of them had suddenly woken from deep sleep. They had each had a similar dream, the substance of which was that William Tennent was in serious trouble and they must go immediately to Trenton to help him. Both fell back to sleep again only to be woken again by the same dreams. When this was repeated a third time, they knew for certain that they must undertake the long journey to Trenton to see what assistance they could give to Tennent. Here then were the very witnesses that he urgently needed, divinely sent, to give credence to the fact that his testimony was true. William Tennent was acquitted. The righteous Judge of all had acted to vindicate his servant. Once again Satan's malice had been thwarted, his evil purposes foiled.

Gilbert

Three sons were born to William Tennent and his wife. Each had received the best education available locally, with two becoming doctors. The third followed his father into the ministry, becoming the pastor of an Independent church in Charleston. Like all Christian parents, William Tennent and his wife followed the careers of their sons with concern and prayer.

The youngest, also named Gilbert, was handsome and popular, and after completing his medical studies had just begun to practice. He had married and had one child. But the young man was wholly indifferent to the spiritual values of his parents, living for nothing except the pleasures that the world could offer him. Earnestly William and his wife pleaded with

God for Gilbert, but no change could they discern in his way of life.

Vaccination against smallpox had not long been introduced and errors with its administration and dosage were an ever-present hazard. As Gilbert was vaccinating patients in a house near his father's home, he himself contracted a fever that proved so virulent that it became clear that he had not long to live. His father seldom left Gilbert's bedside, pleading constantly that God would yet show mercy to his son, even at this final hour. And his prayers were heard. Gilbert's distress of soul became even more severe than his physical pains. At last he became calm as he was given a certainty that his waywardness and sin had been forgiven. Then, even in his extreme illness, Gilbert called for his friends and urged them to seek the mercy of God before they too had to face death. William Tennent, now elderly, took the funeral service for his son and many of Gilbert's young friends heard his exhortations to run to Christ for salvation while opportunity remained.

Return to glory

In 1777, a year in which his country was wracked by war with England—a war that would result in the independence of the colonies—William Tennent, now aged seventy-two, received the call to return to that glory he had glimpsed as a young man. And this time no voice spoke, sending him back into a world of sin, misrepresentation and sorrow.

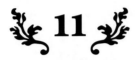

David

A small price to pay

An up-to-date account of a young man's life story from childhood to the present time. David's experiences may well ring many a chord in the lives of others of our generation.

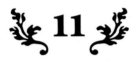

David

A small price to pay

Frightened and fascinated, a six-year-old boy was standing behind a Vulcan bomber aircraft at an RAF annual air display near Norwich. Crowd control was less stringent at the time and the child, who had strayed from his parents, found himself close to the massive bomber as it was preparing to taxi past the admiring crowd. A low whine turned to a shriek and then to a thunderous roar as the engines of the Vulcan fired up in readiness. David could bear no more. In panic he ran to take refuge behind a nearby catering van. But into the six-year-old's mind seeds had been sown of a long-lasting intoxication with aircraft. A love affair had begun—a love affair between the boy and the great masters of the skies. It would influence the entire course of

David's life. What sort of superman would he need to be to sit at the controls of such a magnificent machine as that Vulcan bomber? David determined that one day he would become that superman.

Born in Norwich in 1957, David lived in a small council house with his parents and his brother, Graham, four years his senior. His father was employed as a telephone engineer and his mother helped the family finances by working as a cleaner. Neither had religious interests at that time and David was brought up without any knowledge of God. Yet even as a ten-year-old, thoughts of the inevitability of death, and fear lest it should touch his family circle, would often trouble the child.

Shy, reticent and little interested in academic work, the boy's school reports bore a constant refrain: 'David could do better.' But his teachers little imagined or understood the ambition that was burning inside this quiet child's mind. One day he would become a pilot. One day he would fly those mighty aircraft. All his efforts were concentrated to that one end. He started making balsa wood model planes; then his bedroom became a museum of plastic Airfix models of every type that his pocket money could buy; later these would be succeeded by complex flying models.

Flying

When David was thirteen years of age he took the first steps towards fulfilling his ambitions: he joined the Air Training Corps. Here he received rudimentary instruction in flight techniques, but the progress and opportunities offered to the lad were not enough to satisfy his burning aspirations to train as a pilot. Soon after his sixteenth birthday David joined the Norfolk Gliding Club, financing his all-absorbing interest by a regular paper round and a Saturday job at Debenhams. Now he had his first taste of the delights of flying solo. Such an initial flight was normally quickly followed by a second, accompanied by an experienced man who would check whether the novice was using the controls correctly.

The intervening days between the two flights dragged past for David. Unable to wait until the weekend, the boy decided to abscond from school and present himself at the gliding club. There he managed to persuade an older man to accompany him on his second flight. Impressed by the youth's competence and his degree of self-assurance, David's instructor asked him whether he would like to try some aerobatics. Here was a spirit to match his own; with the older man now at the controls, the glider looped and somersaulted, skimming over houses and fields at a speed of 120 knots and at frighteningly low altitudes. A local dignitary was out for a quiet ride on his horse when suddenly the animal reared into the air as a glider swished over its head, only clearing the nearby hedge by a few feet. David found himself in trouble with the police for the incident and doubtless received a suitable reprimand from his headmaster too.

His future course was becoming clearer in David's own mind. He would need to pass certain subjects at A Level and then he would be in a position to apply to the Royal Air Force to begin training as a pilot. But now the slackness of earlier years was starting to take its toll and even after three years in the sixth form, the young man had only achieved two A Levels. The grades obtained were hardly a solid recommendation to the RAF to accept the new applicant. Undaunted, David went ahead and soon presented himself at the Air Crew Selection Station at Biggin Hill in Kent. At last, the child who had fled in terror at the deafening roar of a Vulcan bomber hoped he might find himself at the controls. Days of intensive testing followed as the young man's reactions were judged in a number of challenging situations. Applicants were expected to possess a wide range of social and leadership skills, and the tall ginger-haired youth from Norwich was shy and uncommunicative.

'You can forget flying, young man,' was the cutting verdict of the chairman of the Selection Board. David turned away, struggling to choke back the tears. Was this to be the end of all his dreams? No! He could not forgo his hopes in such a way. His philosophy of life drove him onwards. This life, he believed, consisted solely of the things one could touch and see—nothing beyond these tangible elements held any relevance for him. Therefore, he would devote all his time and strength into achieving the best that life could offer. For David that meant only one thing: flying aircraft. If the RAF would not train him, he would turn to civil flying. In 1976 when he was nearly nineteen years of age, he applied to British Airways for training as a pilot. Again he received a severe rebuff.

Setbacks
At last David began to come to terms with the thought that he might not be able to achieve his ambition to become a pilot. The best he could hope for at present was to gain his private pilot's licence—by now he had many hours of flying time

behind him—and also to embark on a career in aeronautical engineering. At least he would no longer be creating model aircraft but would be engaged in constructing actual parts of those magnificent machines, the constant focus of his thoughts.

'Don't have anything to do with religion or politics,' was the parting advice David's father gave him as his son set off for London to start his Higher National Diploma in aeronautical engineering at Kingston Polytechnic, as the college was then known. And it was advice that David was happy to follow. But that same year, 1977, David received a telephone call from his brother, Graham, with grievous news. 'Father is dead,' was the blunt message—'killed in a car crash.' David was stunned but unemotional—that father, who like David himself had been a shy and taciturn man and whom he could scarcely say he really knew, was dead, gone, and so suddenly. David hurried home, shocked to the core by the event but also horrified by his own hardness and lack of emotion. He was, however, full of sympathy for the desolation and pain his mother was enduring.

After his return to college David worked well and eventually achieved his HND. When he applied to British Aerospace in the summer of 1979, he was pleased to be given the offer of a job. But wishing to gain further qualifications, he decided to attempt a MSc degree in Aerodynamics at Cranfield Institute of Technology in Bedfordshire. The course had not run for more than a few weeks before David realized that the standard of work was too hard for him. Reluctantly he had to admit to himself that he could never achieve that qualification. At twenty-two years of age his life seemed a story of setbacks and loss. He had been rejected by the RAF, turned down by British Airways, his father had been killed and now there was the realization that the academic work involved in the degree course needed to further his career was beyond his abilities. Perhaps it was these facts that caused David to feel a measure of despair and, on occasions, to drink heavily.

The crisis

The crisis came in October 1979. With a show of bravado David had challenged the timing a fellow student had achieved on an early morning jog. Boasting that he could better his friend's achievement, David set off determined to prove himself the faster runner. But he had drunk eight pints of beer the previous evening and a tot or two of whisky as well. He was in no shape for running. After four hundred yards his left arm began to tingle in a strange way. Instead of stopping, David merely tucked his arm behind his back and continued running. He had not gone much further before his left leg gave way and the young man collapsed in the road. Passing motorists saw the crumpled figure by the roadside and stopped. One look at David's face told them that there was something seriously wrong and they called an ambulance. David had had a massive stroke.

That night in hospital David lay helpless as the medical staff struggled to stabilize his condition. But early the following morning a second stroke left him critically ill. When the hospital notified David's mother of her son's state, she was told that his chances of recovery were slim at best. So soon after the loss of her husband this was a heavy blow. Despite long years with little thought of God, in her despair she telephoned her local vicar to ask for his prayers. And David did pull through. Slowly, very slowly, he began to regain a degree of movement in his leg, though his left arm remained 'as useless as a rag', as he expressed it. 'A stroke is a very humiliating illness at the age of twenty-two,' David confessed. 'I thought only old people had them. Now I was suddenly old.' Wheeled around in a chair because he was unable to walk, David caught sight of himself in a mirror. The distortion in his face—a condition that proved only temporary—filled him with horror. What would his girlfriend say? How would he ever face anyone again? David wished he could die.

After three months the young man began to walk again but with much difficulty, dragging his semi-paralysed leg behind him. He had been told that any degree of recovery he might experience would be made in the first two years; after that his disability would be permanent. Now the strength of David's character and his determination to succeed regardless of setbacks proved an invaluable asset. Hours of exercises were rewarded by a steady improvement in his walking, but his left arm remained totally unresponsive to his best endeavours.

Discharged from hospital early in 1980 David had little idea of what he could do next. With all his hopes shattered, his mind still befuddled from the effects of the stroke, his mobility gone, the future looked bleak indeed. Yet still no thoughts of the God whose wisdom had permitted all these adverse circumstances crossed his mind, although he did find himself strangely attracted to Buddhist concepts. He needed someone to care for him and, after some family pressure, David and the girl he had been courting were married. Financial concerns, David's health and the cramped accommodation he and his wife rented made an inauspicious beginning to married life.

Inauspicious beginning

Courageously, David decided to return to Kingston Polytechnic to make a final attempt to obtain his degree. But the endeavour was doomed from the outset and once more he faced frustration and failure. As the two-year deadline for any significant recovery of mobility approached, David realized that though his walking had improved considerably, he would never regain any use in his left arm. Despair was never far away and already his marriage was faltering. A nadir for the tall, shy youth from Norwich came in October 1981. At the college graduation ceremony David was to receive the HND certificate which he had obtained before his stroke. The hall was crowded for the occasion as parents and students gathered expectantly for the presentations. At last David's turn came to receive his certificate. Dragging his left leg pitifully, the young man struggled to mount the steps on to the platform for no handrail had been provided. Eight hundred pairs of eyes watched his attempts in silence. Then as he stumbled at last on to the platform someone, somewhere, laughed. It was too much; David's spirit snapped. He wept like a child as he walked across to receive his award. At about the same time he experienced the yet harsher pain of remorse as his short-lived marriage collapsed. Full of regrets, David realized that there had been little affection to bind it together.

With every earthly ambition destroyed, every consolation and resting place gone, David wished only for death. How little could he have known at that moment that his real life was about to begin. Eight years earlier he had met a young man who professed to be a Christian. Warm, friendly and full of life, he had impressed David and his consideration for others had remained etched in David's memory. Perhaps there was something in Christianity after all. It was now April 1984 and feeling he had nothing left to lose, he decided he would attend a function organized by the college Christian Union.

No longer alone

'This is a *Christian* Union meeting,' said a student in an incredulous tone as she saw David walking into the room. 'Yes, I know,' replied David quietly as he took his seat in the circle. Describing the cheery hand-clapping and the rousing singing that followed as 'a nasty experience', David was glad when the time came for him to make his escape. But before he left the room someone approached him and invited him to watch a film being shown the following day. With nothing better to do, David accepted the invitation. The film, entitled *No Longer Alone*, told the life story of a woman who had failed as an actress before her eventual conversion. David readily identified with her sense of rejection and loneliness. If Christ had met the needs and despair of the woman in the film, could he not meet his needs also?

The following day there was to be a birthday celebration for one of the members of the Christian Union and again David was invited. Once more he was hoping to make a quick escape when all was over, but before he could do so, one of the group took the opportunity to speak seriously to David, answer his questions and impress upon him his deep spiritual needs. More than this, he offered him the loan of a Bible. Returning to his rooms David began to flick through the pages but had no idea where to start or what to read. His eyes alighted on three words, in fact a paragraph heading in Matthew 5: 'Do not worry.' Only three words, but they were the very ones David needed at that moment. Now he was seriously concerned to understand the message of the Bible.

The next day, a Saturday, David set off to buy himself a Bible in case his new friend wanted his copy back again. As he was about to take the book to the till, he noticed beside it a small booklet with the intriguing title, Mine to Share. Purchasing a copy of that as well (in fact the story of the conversion of the singer, Cliff Richard), David set off back to his room. And in those next hours as he sat reading verse after verse of Scripture, as well as the experiences of Cliff Richard, God met the needy young man, mastered his thinking and convinced him of the truth. He now believed that there was 'a solid case' for the Christian message. But this became more than mere intellectual assent. Secretly, silently the truths of the gospel conquered, convicted and changed David.

That afternoon he set off for Richmond Park. Sitting down in a sunny patch with the world around bright with the hopefulness of a late April day, David continued to read. He looked at the trees. Had he ever really appreciated a tree before? It seemed a new and lovely thing. Young rabbits frisked around him. 'Had God sent them especially,' he wondered. They were so nimble, so full of life. He could truly say with the hymn writer:

> Heaven above is softer blue,
> Earth around is sweeter green;
> Something lives in every hue
> Christless eyes have never seen.
> Birds with gladder songs o'erflow,
> Flowers with deeper beauties shine,
> Since I know, as now I know,
> I am his and he is mine.

A new man

David was indeed a new man in Christ. Where blackness and despair had reigned there was now joy, life and light. On Sunday David's new friends took him to a local evangelical church—the first time he had ever attended a service of worship. Gradually he learnt more about the faith, more about the joys and trials of Christian experience, more about the purposes of God in allowing him to suffer as he had in order to lead him out of his bondage. Now he could join with the congregation and sing from his heart:

> Ransomed, healed, restored, forgiven,
> Who like me his praise should sing?

The following years of David's life must be quickly told. After retraining in computer work at an employment rehabilitation centre, David was offered work experience with British Aerospace. Two weeks of successful work proved that he could hold down a responsible job, managing with one arm what many could not manage with two. He pressed the company to offer him permanent employment, which it did, working there for two years. These years proved invaluable as David gained vital Christian understanding at his local evangelical church. Then came the day when David was asked to move north to work for the British Aerospace's north-eastern division in Brough, near Hull.

Still shy, but now with growing confidence, David quickly settled in his fresh environment and established friendships in his new church. But in Jacky he found the friendship and love of a Christian woman of sterling character.

Their subsequent marriage brought further healing, consolation and richness into David's life. And as a bonus he discovered that Jacky too shared his love of aircraft and was happy to have a large picture of a Phantom bomber decorating the hall in her new home.

Growing in his usefulness in the church, David became a deacon. After some years he left British Aerospace and now serves God, together with Jacky, at the Spanish Gospel Mission House in Valdepeñas, Spain. But looking back on all the pain and frustration of his pathway, he once declared, 'It was a small price to pay for all the blessings of salvation.'

Bibliography and suggested further reading

William Mackay
Grace and Truth, Edinburgh, 1890.
The Seeking Saviour, Hodder & Stoughton, 1904.

William Clowes
Joseph Ritson, *The Romance of Primitive Methodism*, London,
1909 (downloadable from http://quintapress.macmate.me/
PDF_Books/Romance.pdf)
John Wilkinson, *William Clowes*, Epworth Press, 1951.

Grace Bennet
Samuel Burder, *Memoirs of Eminently Pious Women*, vol. ii,
London, 1815.

Thomas Lee
J. Telford, ed., *Wesley's Veterans*, vol. iii, Epworth Press, 1912.

Joan Waste and William Hunter
John Fox, *Book of Martyrs*, vol. iii, ed. John Cummings, London, 1875.

John Vanderkemp
A. D. Martin, *Doctor Vanderkemp*, Livingstone Press.

Marion Veitch
Memoirs of Mrs William Veitch, Edinburgh, 1846.
Kenneth W. H. Howard, *Marion Veitch*, Gospel Tidings Trust, 1992.

John Cennick
Village Discourses, with a Life of the Author, Halifax, 1862.
V. W. Couillard, *Transactions of the Moravian Historical Society*, Ph.D. thesis, Moravian Historical Society Pennsylvania, 1957.
A. Dallimore, *George Whitefield, The Life and Times of the Great Evangelist of the 18th Century Revival*, vols 1 & 2, London and Edinburgh, Banner of Truth Trust, 1970 & 1980.

Ruth Clark
M. P. Hack, *Faithful Service, Sketches of Christian Women*, Hodder & Stoughton, 1885.
Letters of Henry Venn, Edinburgh, Banner of Truth Trust, 1993.

William Tennent
Archibald Alexander, *The Log College*, London, Banner of Truth Trust, 1968.